THE ULTIMATE
SAN JOSE SHARKS
TRIVIA BOOK

A Collection of Amazing Trivia Quizzes
and Fun Facts for Die-Hard Sharks Fans!

Ray Walker

Exclusive Free Book

Crazy Sports Stories

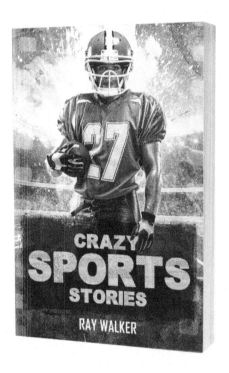

As a thank you for getting a copy of this book I would like to offer you a free copy of my book Crazy Sports Stories which comes packed with interesting stories from your favorite sports such as Football, Hockey, Baseball, Basketball and more.

**Grab your free copy over at
RayWalkerMedia.com/Bonus**

CONTENTS

INTRODUCTION

The San Jose Sharks became an instant hit with hockey fans upon joining the NHL in 1991-92 because of their entertaining style and never-say-die attitude.

Even though they set an NHL record for futility in only their second season, when they lost 71 games, they were still a fascinating bunch to their fans.

The team improved by an incredible 58 points in its third campaign and made the playoffs for the first time. Once there, they disposed of the heavily favored Detroit Red Wings in seven games before falling to Toronto in another seven-game set.

The Sharks' fortunes began to turn and, as of 2019-20, they have made the playoffs in 21 of 28 seasons. The Stanley Cup is still missing from the club's list of achievements after losing in six games to Pittsburgh in the 2015-16 final series, but they have won a Presidents' Trophy as the NHL's top regular-season squad as well as a conference championship and six division titles.

With a loyal and passionate fan base, the Sharks survived the lean years before showing some teeth and becoming one of the NHL's most consistent clubs. From the early days of the Cow Palace to the SAP Center, San Jose fans are still treated to some of the league's best hockey. They've seen some of the league's best players wear the uniform, such as Teemu Selanne, Rob Blake, Brent Burns, Joe Thornton, Patrick Marleau, Joe Pavelski, Jonathan Cheechoo, Erik Karlsson, and goaltender Evgeni Nabokov.

This San Jose Sharks trivia and factbook is overflowing with an assortment of trivia facts about the franchise from day one to the end of the 2019-20 regular NHL season.

It contains 15 different sections, each containing 15 multiple-choice and five true-or-false questions, with the answers being revealed on a later page. Each quiz chapter also reveals 10 historical "Did You Know" facts about the franchise's players, coaches, general managers, ownership, etc.

Sharks supporters can refresh their memories and relive the team's history with the book and perhaps even pick up some new information while doing so. It's the perfect research tool to help prepare yourself for contests and trivia challenges against fellow San Jose fans.

Hopefully, you'll enjoy this journey through time and reaffirm yourself standing as a solid Sharks supporter.

CHAPTER 1:

ORIGINS & HISTORY

QUIZ TIME!

1. How much was the NHL expansion fee to land a franchise in San Jose?

    a. $55 million

    b. $60 million

    c. $50 million

    d. $75 million

2. Who was the club's first coach?

    a. Kevin Constantine

    b. Jim Wiley

    c. Al Sims

    d. George Kingston

3. In their first season, Sharks' merchandise sales ranked second among all North American pro sports teams behind the Chicago Bulls.

    a. True

    b. False

4. Which of the following team names was not considered when branding the franchise?

    a. Golden Gaters

    b. Redwoods

    c. Golden Waves

    d. Icebreakers

5. The Sharks made their NHL debut against which team?

    a. Detroit Red Wings

    b. Vancouver Canucks

    c. Edmonton Oilers

    d. Chicago Blackhawks

6. What arena did the Sharks play in for their first two seasons?

    a. Cow Palace

    b. San Jose Arena

    c. Oakland Coliseum Arena

    d. Nazareth Oasis Arena

7. Against which team did the Sharks' first victory come?

    a. Winnipeg Jets

    b. Calgary Flames

    c. Minnesota North Stars

    d. Boston Bruins

8. The Sharks were the only NHL expansion team to debut in the 1991-92 season.

    a. True

    b. False

9. How many games did the Sharks lose in their inaugural season?

    a. 25

    b. 61

    c. 35

    d. 58

10. When did San Jose make their first playoff appearance?

    a. 1992-93

    b. 1995-96

    c. 1994-95

    d. 1993-94

11. The club was the 21st franchise to join the NHL.

    a. True

    b. False

12. Gordon and George Gund were minority owners of which NHL team before founding the Sharks?

    a. Detroit Red Wings

    b. Hartford Whalers

    c. Minnesota North Stars

    d. Buffalo Sabres

13. Who scored the first goal in Sharks' history?

    a. Brian Mullen

    b. Pat MacLeod

    c. Doug Wilson

    d. Craig Coxe

14. The club made its first Stanley Cup final appearance in 2015-16.

    a. True
    b. False

15. Who led the team in points in its debut campaign?

    a. Kelly Kisio
    b. Brian Lawton
    c. Pat Falloon
    d. David Bruce

16. Who was the first player selected by the club in the 1991 NHL dispersal draft?

    a. Brian Hayward
    b. Shane Churla
    c. Neil Wilkinson
    d. Rob Zettler

17. How many seasons did the Sharks spend in the Smythe Division?

    a. 2
    b. 4
    c. 3
    d. 1

18. How many games did the squad win in its inaugural season?

    a. 12
    b. 20
    c. 17
    d. 14

19. The Sharks hold the record for most losses in an NHL season with how many?

   a. 68
   b. 71
   c. 65

20. 70

21. In its first season, the team scored the fewest and conceded the most goals in the NHL.

   a. True
   b. False

QUIZ ANSWERS

1. C – $50 million

2. D – George Kingston

3. A – True

4. C – Golden Waves

5. B – Vancouver Canucks

6. A – Cow Palace

7. B – Calgary Flames

8. A – True

9. D – 58

10. D – 1993-94

11. B – False

12. C – Minnesota North Stars

13. D – Craig Coxe

14. A – True

15. C – Pat Falloon

16. B – Shane Churla

17. A – 2

18. C – 17

19. B – 71

20. A – True

DID YOU KNOW?

1. The San Jose Sharks NHL franchise is based in the city of San Jose, California, in the USA. The club made its NHL debut in the 1991-92 season, when the league expanded from 21 to 22 teams, and currently competes in the Pacific Division in the league's Western Conference. The Sharks' minor league affiliate is the San Jose Barracuda of the American Hockey League (AHL).

2. The franchise was awarded on May 9, 1990, at a cost of $50 million and became the first NHL club based in the San Francisco Bay area of California since the California Golden Seals left in 1976 to relocate in Ohio as the Cleveland Barons. The Golden Seals originally joined the NHL as the Oakland Seals in 1967-68.

3. The Sharks' franchise is currently owned by a private firm known as San Jose Sports & Entertainment Enterprises. The company, which was founded in 2002, also owns the San Jose Barracuda AHL franchise, is a minority owner of the San Jose Earthquakes MLS soccer club, and manages the SAP Center arena in San Jose.

4. The owners of San Jose Sports & Entertainment Enterprises are Hasso Plattner, Gordon Russell, Rudy Staedler, and Gary Valenzuela. The company purchased the Sharks' franchise from George Gund III and Gordon Gund in 2002 on the condition that the team remained in

San Jose. The Gunds were previous minority owners of the California Golden Seals and Minnesota North Stars.

5. The Gunds originally asked the NHL if they could relocate the Minnesota North Stars to the San Jose area in the late 1980s. However, the league turned down the request. At the same time, Harold Baldwin, former owner of the Hartford Whalers NHL franchise, also wanted to bring a team to San Jose because a new arena was being built. The NHL proposed that the Gunds sell their interest in the North Stars to Baldwin and they would be awarded a franchise for San Jose.

6. More than 5,000 potential names for the San Jose franchise were sent in by mail in a contest, with "The Blades" being the winner. However, the Gunds believed the name could be associated negatively with weapons. The Sharks, which was the runner-up in the contest, was then chosen.

7. The Sharks played their home games at the Cow Palace in Daly City for their first two seasons. Ironically, the California Golden Seals and the NHL rejected this rink as a suitable venue when the Seals entered the league in 1967.

8. In 1992-93, the Sharks lost an NHL record 71 games and endured a 17-match losing streak while earning just 24 points and 11 wins. Even so, the club led the league in merchandise sales at $150 million, which represented 27% of the NHL's total sales. In addition, the team recorded its first shutout in 1992–93 and first hat trick.

9. In 1993-94, the club moved to the San Jose Arena (now the SAP Center) and also moved from the Smythe Division to

the Pacific Division. The team also made the playoffs for the first time, improving by an NHL record 58 points from the season before.

10. As of 2019-20, the Sharks had yet to win a Stanley Cup. They reached the final in 2015-16 but were beaten in six games by the Pittsburgh Penguins. However, the franchise has won six division championships, one conference championship, and one Presidents' Trophy.

CHAPTER 2:

JERSEYS & NUMBERS

QUIZ TIME!

1. Who was the first goalie to wear No. 1 with the club?

    a. Ed Belfour

    b. Jeff Hackett

    c. Brian Hayward

    d. Thomas Greiss

2. What number did Andrew Desjardins wear in his first two seasons with the team?

    a. 10

    b. 12

    c. 69

    d. 76

3. As of 2019, the Sharks have updated their primary logo once.

    a. True

    b. False

4. When did the Sharks add a black alternate jersey?

   a. 2000-01
   b. 2001-02
   c. 2002-03
   d. 2003-04

5. What number did Owen Nolan wear for eight seasons in San Jose?

   a. 18
   b. 21
   c. 88
   d. 11

6. Who wore No. 5 from 2013 to 2015?

   a. Raffi Torres
   b. Martin Havlát
   c. Jason Demers
   d. Douglas Murray

7. As of 2019, how many unique jerseys have the Sharks worn for special events?

   a. 1
   b. 3
   c. 0
   d. 2

8. The triangle featured on the Sharks logo references the "Red Triangle" in the Bay Area, which is known for its shark population.

   a. True
   b. False

9. Which number has not been worn by a Sharks player, as of 2019-20?

    a. 77
    b. 75
    c. 65
    d. 34

10. Who wore No. 20 from 2003 to 2010?

    a. Ryane Clowe
    b. Mark Smith
    c. Evgeni Nabokov
    d. Scott Hannan

11. In 2007-08, the Sharks added a yellow accent color to their jerseys.

    a. True
    b. False

12. Who was the first player to wear No. 61 for the Sharks?

    a. Justin Braun
    b. Andrei Nazarov
    c. Kevin Labanc
    d. Derick Joslin

13. Which number did Doug Wilson wear in his two seasons with the club?

    a. 20
    b. 22
    c. 44
    d. 24

14. The highest number worn by a member of the Sharks is 92.

    a. True
    b. False

15. What color did the Sharks stop using in their jerseys in 2006-07?

    a. Red
    b. Gray
    c. Blue
    d. Orange

16. Who wore No. 18 from 1998 to 2004?

    a. Niko Dimitrakos
    b. Marco Sturm
    c. Mike Ricci
    d. Scott Thornton

17. What number did Joel Ward wear while in San Jose?

    a. 29
    b. 32
    c. 27
    d. 42

18. Who was the first Sharks player to wear No. 74?

    a. Freddie Hamilton
    b. Matthew Nieto
    c. Dylan DeMelo
    d. Tyler Kennedy

19. How many players have worn No. 43 as of 2019-20?

    a. 9

    b. 10

    c. 12

    d. 7

20. Brent Burns was the first player on the team to wear No. 88.

    a. True

    b. False

QUIZ ANSWERS

1. C – Brian Hayward

2. C – 69

3. A – True

4. B – 2001-02

5. D – 11

6. C – Jason Demers

7. D – 2

8. A – True

9. A – 77

10. C – Evgeni Nabokov

11. B – False

12. A – Justin Braun

13. D – 24

14. B – False

15. B – Gray

16. C – Mike Ricci

17. D – 42

18. C – Dylan DeMelo

19. A – 9

20. A – True

DID YOU KNOW?

1. The Sharks' home jersey is predominantly deep Pacific teal with black and white trimming. The away jersey is mainly white with black and silver trim. There is also an alternate jersey that is predominantly black with teal trim. The team wears black pants with each jersey and the socks are the same primary color as the jersey being worn.

2. The franchise logo, which features a shark biting a hockey stick, has been in use since the team entered the league. There were slight modifications in 2007. There is also a triangle in the logo that refers to the Red Triangle area in the nearby Pacific Ocean. In addition, the club uses a variety of alternate and partial logos which are based on its primary logo.

3. San Jose has introduced alternate jerseys and at times has made slight modifications to the home and away uniforms and logos. This includes a tri-color teal, black, and white that was worn for the 2015 NHL Stadium Series.

4. The San Jose Sharks organization has yet to officially retire any jersey numbers. However, the NHL retired No. 99 at the league's All-Star Game in 2000 to honor its all-time leading scorer, Wayne Gretzky.

5. The most popular sweater numbers in team history so far have been 5, 9, and 26, with a dozen players wearing each number as of 2019-20. Those wearing No. 5 include Doug Bodger and Jeff Norton while Bernie Nicholls and Evander

Kane have worn No. 9 and Steve Bernie and Michal Handzuš have donned No. 26.

6. Every number from 1 to 55 has been worn at least once throughout the team's history. In addition, 28 different numbers from 57 to 94 have been worn. The highest, No. 94, was worn by Alexander Korolyuk in 2004.

7. No. 13, which is considered to be bad luck in certain cultures around the world, has been worn by five different Sharks. They are Rick Lessard, Jamie Baker, Todd Harvey, Bill Guerin, and Raffi Torres. However, it hasn't been worn since Torres in 2013-14.

8. Although the No. 1 jersey has long been associated with goaltenders, just two Sharks' netminders have worn the digit. Brian Hayward was the first to don it from 1992 to 1993 and Thomas Greiss eventually took it over from 2008 to 2013.

9. Perhaps surprisingly, the Nos. 43 and 47 have also been popular with San Jose players. Nine members of the team have worn 43 while eight have skated with 47 on their backs. Those wearing 43 include Ray Whitney, Al Iafrate, and Scott Hannan, while Mike Sullivan, Yves Racine, and Darren Turcotte have worn 47.

10. The Sharks' all-time scoring leader, Patrick Marleau, wore two different numbers with the club. He donned No. 14 from 1997 to 2001 and then switched to No. 12 from 2002 to 2017 before signing with Toronto as a free agent. He also wore No. 12 when he returned to San Jose in 2019-20 before being traded to Pittsburgh in February 2020.

CHAPTER 3:

FAMOUS QUOTES

QUIZ TIME!

1. Which free agent was GM Doug Wilson speaking about in 2005 when he said, "We take it as a compliment how our team is viewed by a high-end player"?

   a. Scott Niedermayer

   b. Alexander Mogilny

   c. Ed Jovanovski

   d. Zdeno Chára

2. Which former Shark and high-scoring NHL player once said, "I'm an old-school guy. I don't try to be too flashy"?

   a. Patrick Marleau

   b. Dany Heatley

   c. Mike Ricci

   d. Bernie Nicholls

3. Joe Thornton was alluding to retirement in 2019-20 when he said, "As you get older, you realize you only have so many shots at this thing, and it would have been nice to have a chance"?

a. True

b. False

4. Which Sharks forward commented, "I'm just an average Canadian kid playing hockey"?

   a. Jamie Baker

   b. Devin Setoguchi

   c. Todd Harvey

   d. Joe Thornton

5. Which former Shark stated, "Games in hand are a good thing only if you win them"?

   a. Coach Darryl Sutter

   b. Patrick Marleau

   c. Coach Ron Wilson

   d. Gustav Nyquist

6. "I may not know much but I can count," was once said by which San Jose head coach?

   a. Todd McLellan

   b. Jim Wiley

   c. Darryl Sutter

   d. Pete DeBoer

7. Which general manager liked to say, "Every good army needs a couple of criminals"?

   a. Doug Wilson

   b. Jack Ferreira

   c. Dean Lombardi

   d. Chuck Grillo

8. Following a loss to Dallas in 2005-06, Jonathan Cheechoo said, "It just goes to show, even when you have the effort it's hard to win in this league."

   a. True
   b. False

9. Who was Brent Burns speaking about in 2015 when he said, "The guy is just such an unbelievable human and a great teammate"?

   a. Joe Thornton
   b. Patrick Marleau
   c. Joe Pavelski
   d. Martin Jones

10. Which general manager once claimed, "Everyone has to be singing from the same hymn book"?

   a. Doug Wilson
   b. Dean Lombardi
   c. Chuck Grillo
   d. Jack Ferreira

11. Former MLB player Nyjer Morgan once said, "That's basically Mr. San Jose Shark..." about ex-Shark Owen Nolan.

   a. True
   b. False

12. "The expectation is always going to be winning a Stanley Cup, so it's disappointing anytime you fall short of that." Which goaltender said this?

a. Martin Jones

b. Ed Belfour

c. Thomas Greiss

d. Aaron Dell

13. Who replied, "Not great" when asked about the team's culture in April 2015?

a. Logan Couture

b. Coach Todd McLellan

c. Brent Burns

d. Joe Thornton

14. San Jose's Teemu Selanne famously said this about Sharks' coach Ron Wilson: "He isn't my favorite coach anymore."

a. True

b. False

15. After losing in the 2017 playoffs, who said, "Old age has nothing to do with it. Marleau is 37 and he's one of the fastest guys in the league"?

a. Coach Pete DeBoer

b. General manager Doug Wilson

c. Marc-Edouard Vlasic

d. Brent Burns

16. Who was head coach Pete DeBoer referring to in 2017 when he stated, "We're expecting big things out of him next year. We need him to take a step"?

a. Joonas Donskoi

b. Mikkel Boedker

c. Joel Ward

d. Justin Braun

17. Which opponent was Bernie Nicholls speaking about when he said, "You're always aware of him physically. He's the best we play against"?

    a. Matt Johnson

    b. Sean O'Donnell

    c. Kevin Stevens

    d. Rob Blake

18. Which Shark was once quoted as saying, "Confidence is everything in this sport. When you're confident, you're playing your best"?

    a. Chris Tierney

    b. Paul Martin

    c. c. Tomas Hertl

    d. d. Mikkel Boedker

19. Which Shark made this comment: "It's hard to play center. You have to be strong all over the ice. I'm learning still"?

    a. Patrick Marleau

    b. Joe Pavelski

    c. Melker Karlsson

    d. Tomáš Hertl

20. Sharks' goalie Antti Niemi once said, "We won't win many games if we don't score more goals than they do."

    a. True

    b. False

QUIZ ANSWERS

1. A – Scott Niedermayer

2. B – Dany Heatley

3. B – False

4. D – Joe Thornton

5. B – Patrick Marleau

6. C – Darryl Sutter

7. C – Dean Lombardi

8. B – False

9. A – Joe Thornton

10. B – Dean Lombardi

11. A – True

12. A – Martin Jones

13. A – Logan Couture

14. A – True

15. C – Marc-Edouard Vlasic

16. B – Mikkel Boedker

17. D – Rob Blake

18. D – Mikkel Boedker

19. D – Tomáš Hertl

20. False

DID YOU KNOW?

1. When the franchise decided on the name Sharks, the club's marketing head Matt Levine remarked, "Sharks are relentless, determined, swift, agile, bright, and fearless. We plan to build an organization that has all those qualities."

2. When ace defender Scott Niedermayer left New Jersey as a free agent in 2005, he was close to signing with San Jose. However, he chose Anaheim instead to play with his brother Rob. At the time he stated, "Since he was 15 and I was 16 we've been apart playing hockey, and now we're going to get an opportunity to be on the same team."

3. Former Sharks forward Dany Heatley once said, when explaining what it was like being a pro hockey player, "You do your job, you get your work done at the rink and then you go home. The big thing is figuring out what you're going to do the rest of the day."

4. Describing the feeling for a Sharks' home game, Joe Thornton commented, "You don't realize the atmosphere in the arena until you're down on the ice, especially during the playoffs. You come out of the gate, you hear the fans going crazy, you know you're at home and in for a good time. It's something special, that's for sure."

5. Patrick Marleau, the top scorer in team history once chimed in by saying, "I can't control what people say or anything like that. I have to focus on what I can control and that's what I'm going to do."

6. After an especially rough day, former Shark's coach Darryl Sutter complained to the media, "It has not been a good day. I lost my glasses early this morning and I had to go buy a pair of 79 dollar reading glasses today. 79 bucks. You can literally get them at Costco, three-for-20."

7. Former San Jose general manager Dean Lombardi had this to say about players being on the cover of a famous hockey publication: "First of all, it's a curse. Voodoo. As soon as a guy gets put on the cover of *The Hockey News*, it's like *Sports Illustrated*. He goes right into the tank."

8. High-scoring blue-liner Brent Burns said this about also playing forward during his NHL career, "You j ust turn your brain off and turn your legs on. Have fun, no stress, then go back to 'D,' turn the brain on and you've got to start thinking again."

9. When the Sharks blew a 3-0 series lead over Los Angeles in the first round of the 2013-14 playoffs, general manager Doug Wilson described his team's performance "like Charlie Brown trying to kick a football." It was just the fourth time in NHL history a team had lost a seven-game series after winning the first three contests.

10. Following an early exit in the 2016-17 postseason, head coach Pete DeBoer stated, "I feel we had a team that could compete for a Stanley Cup this year and I felt that all year. I felt that even going into Game 6 of the series against Edmonton. To be sitting here on the outside is disappointing. I felt we had a better team than that. The

message to the group is they individually have to look in the mirror on what they can do so we don't feel like this again next year."

CHAPTER 4:

CATCHY NICKNAMES

QUIZ TIME!

1. Which player is famously known as "Jumbo"?

    a. Pat Falloon

    b. Dave Brown

    c. Brenden Dillon

    d. Joe Thornton

2. Who is referred to as "Pickles" or "Pickle Jar"?

    a. Chris Tierney

    b. Marc-Edouard Vlasic

    c. Aaron Dell

    d. Joonas Donskoi

3. Patrick Marleau is the one and only "Mr. Shark."

    a. True

    b. False

4. Which Sharks coach was dubbed "The Jolly Rancher"?

    a. Todd McLellan

    b. Darryl Sutter

   c. George Kingston

   d. Peter DeBoer

5. What was Bryan Marchment's nickname?

   a. Captain Crush

   b. Boards

   c. Mush

   d. Rocky

6. This former Sharks' player was known as "The Sheriff."

   a. Ron Sutter

   b. Craig Rivet

   c. James Sheppard

   d. Jeff Odgers

7. What simple nickname did Jeremy Roenick have during his career?

   a. Nicky

   b. J.R

   c. Rose

   d. Jay

8. The club earned the nickname "The Fins" because of their secondary logo of a shark fin.

   a. True

   b. False

9. Which of the following is not one of Brent Burns' nicknames?

   a. Sasquatch

   b. Wookie

c. Burnsie

d. Chewbacca

10. What is star defenseman Erik Karlsson's nickname?

    a. The Lighter

    b. Kartman

    c. The Swede

    d. King Karl

11. Owen Nolan was known as "Buster."

    a. True

    b. False

12. Which player was known as "The Big Cheese"?

    a. Dany Heatley

    b. Tommy Wingels

    c. Joel Ward

    d. Raffi Torres

13. Which one isn't a nickname that Logan Couture has gone by?

    a. Loco

    b. Loggy

    c. Clutch

    d. Clutchure

14. Link Gaetz was nicknamed "The Missing Link."

    a. True

    b. False

15. What was Evgeni Nabokov's moniker?

    a. Nabsy

    b. Geni

    c. Kovy

    d. Nabby

16. Who was known as "Captain America"?

    a. Matt Nieto

    b. Joe Pavelski

    c. Justin Braun

    d. Ryan Carpenter

17. What is not one of Martin Jones' nicknames?

    a. J–Onesie

    b. Joner

    c. Game of Jones

    d. Jonesy

18. Who was nicknamed "Heater"?

    a. Dany Heatley

    b. Freddie Hamilton

    c. Shawn Heins

    d. Michal Handzuš

19. Igor Larionov was known by which nickname?

    a. The Artist

    b. The Sniper

    c. The Professor

    d. The Surgeon

20. Evander Kane is called "Candy Kane" by teammates.

    a. True
    b. False

QUIZ ANSWERS

1. D – Joe Thornton

2. B – Marc-Edouard Vlasic

3. B – True

4. B – Darryl Sutter

5. C – Mush

6. D – Jeff Odgers

7. B – J.R

8. A – True

9. A – Sasquatch

10. D – King Karl

11. A – True

12. C – Joel Ward

13. B – Loggy

14. A – True

15. D – Nabby

16. B – Joe Pavelski

17. A – J–Onesie

18. A – Dany Heatley

19. C – The Professor

20. B – False

DID YOU KNOW?

1. The city of San Jose is often called "The capital of Silicon Valley," "San Jo," "Teal Town," "Fin City," and "Garden City." The official nickname for the state of California is "The Golden State." The hockey team has been called several names such as "Fins," "Fish," "The Teal Team," "Team Teal," "Tuna," and "The Men of Teal.' In addition, the SAP Center is nicknamed "The Shark Tank."

2. Goaltender Ed Belfour was known by several similar nicknames, which were "The Eagle," "Eddie the Eagle," "Crazy Eddie" and "Eddie the Billionaire." He was known as "The Eagle" due to the graphic on his recognizable facemask and as "Crazy Eddie" because of his somewhat bizarre off-ice antics. Belfour played for San Jose in 1996-97.

3. The Sharks' popular blue-liner Brent Burns is also known by more than one moniker. His most common nicknames since breaking into the NHL in 2005 are "Burnsie," "The Wookie," and "Chewbacca." Burns joined San Jose before the 2011-12 season.

4. Rearguard Marc-Edouard Vlasic earned the nickname "Pickles" at one of his first training camps with th e team and it stuck. However, it was voted one of the worst monikers on the squad by his teammates in an informal 2018 poll. Vlasic was drafted by the organization in 2005 and was still a member as of 2019-20.

5. The favorite nickname with Sharks' players according to their 2018 poll was "The Cobra," which was bestowed upon Chris Tierney. The center was drafted by the Sharks in 2012 and played with the club between 2014 and 2018 before being dealt to Ottawa.

6. Defender Brian Campbell, who made his NHL debut with Buffalo in 1999-2000, was nicknamed "Soupy" and "Rusty." The nickname "Soupy" came about due to having the same name as the famous Campbell Soup Company. He played briefly for the Sharks in 2007-08.

7. Goaltender Aaron Dell was given the nickname "Dell-icious" by teammate Joe Thornton as a play on words regarding his last name. He's also known as "Lala" by teammates. Dell was undrafted and signed with San Jose as a free agent, making his NHL debut in October 2016. He was still with the club in 2019-20.

8. Forward Joe Thornton himself is known as "Jumbo Joe" and "Big Joe" with the nicknames being due to his 6-foot-4-inch, 220-pound frame. Thornton was given the monikers while with the Boston Bruins, where he played from 1997 to 2005 before being traded to San Jose. The legendary Shark was still with the team in 2019-20.

9. When right-winger Mikkel Boedker was taken eighth overall in the 2008 NHL Draft by Phoenix, he became the highest-drafted Danish-born player in history. He signed a four-year, $16 million deal with San Jose in 2016 and was known by teammates as "Hot Boed." He played two years

with the team before being traded to Ottawa and then left the NHL to play in Switzerland in 2020.

10. Current San Jose captain Logan Couture is known by several nicknames, which are "Cooch," "LoCo," "Juicy," "Clutchure" and "Clutch." He was drafted in the first round by the club in 2007 and named the captain before the 2019-20 campaign. He's certainly earned the moniker "Clutch" by notching 101 points in 116 playoff games as of 2020.

CHAPTER 5:

THE CAPTAIN CLASS

QUIZ TIME!

1. Who was the first captain of the Sharks?

    a. Bob Errey

    b. Doug Wilson

    c. David Williams

    d. Kelly Kisio

2. What is the most goals scored in one season by a captain?

    a. 41

    b. 34

    c. 44

    d. 38

3. Patrick Marleau was the youngest player to captain the Sharks.

    a. True

    b. False

4. How old was Patrick Marleau when he became captain?

    a. 22
    b. 23
    c. 24
    d. 25

5. Which player has the most assists in a season as captain?

    a. Vincent Damphousse
    b. Joe Pavelski
    c. Owen Nolan
    d. Joe Thornton

6. Which captain went a full season without scoring a goal?

    a. Rob Blake
    b. Mike Ricci
    c. Bob Errey
    d. Todd Gill

7. What is the most penalty minutes a captain has recorded in a season?

    a. 192
    b. 129
    c. 177
    d. 126

8. Bob Errey and Todd Gill shared the captaincy in 1994-95.

    a. True
    b. False

9. Who wore the "C" in 2009-10?

   a. Rob Blake

   b. Joe Thornton

   c. Scott Nichol

   d. Joe Pavelski

10. Which player was not an alternate captain in 2019-20?

   a. Brent Burns

   b. Tomas Hertl

   c. Marc-Edouard Vlasic

   d. Erik Karlsson

11. Jeff Odgers played the fewest games in a season as captain, as he was traded after 13 games.

   a. True

   b. False

12. Who was named captain in 2019?

   a. Erik Karlsson

   b. Logan Couture

   c. Joe Thornton

   d. Evander Kane

13. Who served as skipper from 1998 to 2003?

   a. Mike Rathje

   b. Jim Montgomery

   c. Owen Nolan

   d. Gary Sutter

14. The Sharks used a rotating captain system in 2003-04.

    a. True
    b. False

15. Who did not serve as captain in 2003-04?

    a. Patrick Marleau
    b. Alyn McCauley
    c. Mike Ricci
    d. Jonathan Cheechoo

16. Which season did the club go without a captain?

    a. 2013-14
    b. 2012-13
    c. 2015-16
    d. 2014-15

17. Rob Blake was the oldest captain of the Sharks at what age?

    a. 39
    b. 40
    c. 38
    d. 42

18. What is the highest plus/minus rating recorded in a single campaign by a Sharks' captain?

    a. +29
    b. -34
    c. +25
    d. -30

19. What is the fewest penalty minutes recorded by a captain in one season?

    a. 24

    b. 20

    c. 15

    d. 18

20. Joe Pavelski was the longest-serving skipper of the team.

    a. True

    b. False

QUIZ ANSWERS

1. B – Doug Wilson

2. C – 44

3. A – True

4. C – 24

5. D – Joe Thornton

6. D – Todd Gill

7. A – 192

8. B – False

9. A – Rob Blake

10. C – Marc-Edouard Vlasic

11. B – False

12. B – Logan Couture

13. C – Owen Nolan

14. A – True

15. D – Jonathan Cheechoo

16. D – 2014-15

17. B – 40

18. C – +25

19. D – 18

20. B – False

DID YOU KNOW?

1. The Sharks have appointed 13 different players as captain since entering the NHL. Doug Wilson was the first, followed by Bob Errey, Jeff Odgers, Todd Gill, Owen Nolan, Mike Ricci, Vincent Damphousse, Alyn McCauley, Patrick Marleau, Rob Blake, Joe Thornton, Joe Pavelski, and Logan Couture, who took over in 2019.

2. San Jose employed a lone captain in every season except 2003-04 and 2014-15. There was no skipper in 2014-15 and in 2003-04 they used a rotating system for the first half of the campaign. Mike Ricci wore the "C" for the first 10 games, followed by Vincent Damphousse for 20 games and Alyn McCauley for 20 contests. Patrick Marleau then took over until the end of the 2008-09 campaign.

3. Bob Errey was the Sharks' skipper in 1994-95 until being traded to Detroit in February 1995. When Errey departed, the captaincy was taken over by undrafted Jeff Odgers for the remainder of the season and for the 1995-96 campaign.

4. The highest-scoring season by a team captain was registered by Patrick Marleau in 2005-06, when he racked up 34 goals and 86 points in 82 contests. Fellow forward Owen Nolan was a close second in 1999-2000 when he posted 44 goals and 84 points.

5. San Jose captains have been assessed more than 100 penalty minutes in one season on six occasions. Jeff

Odgers leads the way with 192 minutes in 1995-96, followed by Owen Nolan with 129 in 1998-99, Bob Errey with 126 in 1993-94, Odgers again with 117 minutes in 1994-95, Nolan with 110 in 1999-2000, and Todd Gill with 101 minutes in 1996-97.

6. The longest-serving Sharks captain was Owen Nolan, who was born in Belfast, Northern Ireland. He was appointed for the 1998-99 campaign and held the job for almost five complete seasons until being traded to Toronto in March 2003.

7. When Owen Nolan was traded to the Maple Leafs late in the 2002-03 season, the Sharks received center Alyn McCauley as part of the package. McCauley served as one of the team's rotating captains the next season and posted 83 points in 174 regular-season games before signing as a free agent with Los Angeles in 2006.

8. One of the Sharks' most unsung skippers was defender Todd Gill who wore the "C" for two seasons from 1996 to 1998. Gill was acquired from Toronto in a June 1996 trade and was given the captaincy shortly afterward. He played 143 regular-season outings and chipped in with 42 points before being traded to St. Louis in March 1998. He played close to 20 years in the NHL with seven different clubs and appeared in 1,007 regular-season contests.

9. Forward Joe Pavelski was a long-time Shark who was drafted in 2003 with the 205th overall pick. He skated with the team from 2006-07 until signing with Dallas as a free

agent in 2019. Pavelski acted as Sharks' captain for four seasons, from 2015 until his departure. He left San Jose with 355 goals and 761 points in 963 games and added 48 goals and 100 points in 134 postseason encounters.

10. The youngest captain in Sharks' history was Patrick Marleau, who was 24 years old in the 2003-04 season. The oldest was blue-liner Rob Blake, who was 40 years of age during the 2009-10 campaign, which was his second of two seasons with the club and his last in the NHL.

CHAPTER 6:

STATISTICALLY SPEAKING

QUIZ TIME!

1. Which player is the franchise leader in assists as of 2020?

   a. Joe Thornton

   b. Patrick Marleau

   c. Owen Nolan

   d. Brent Burns

2. The Sharks have scored how many goals on 55 regular-season penalty shots?

   a. 25

   b. 14

   c. 23

   d. 21

3. Joe Pavelski has scored the most career power-play goals in the regular season.

   a. True

   b. False

4. Jonathan Cheechoo holds the record for the most regular-season hat tricks with how many?

    a. 6

    b. 4

    c. 7

    d. 5

5. How many goals did the Sharks score in their 2015-16 Stanley Cup run?

    a. 72

    b. 59

    c. 75

    d. 67

6. What is the most games played by a Sharks' goalie in a single season?

    a. 68

    b. 56

    c. 72

    d. 77

7. In what season did the Sharks record a franchise-best 53 wins?

    a. 2009-10

    b. 2008-09

    c. 2016-17

    d. 2015-16

8. Joe Pavelski had a single-season shooting percentage of 20.2% in 2018-19.

a. True

b. False

9. What is the most minutes played by a Sharks goalie in a single regular season?

    a. 3,936

    b. 4,194

    c. 4,412

    d. 4,561

10. How many regular-season hat tricks have Sharks players scored as of 2019-20?

    a. 53

    b. 58

    c. 66

    d. 71

11. Jeff Odgers had 1,001 career penalty minutes with the Sharks.

    a. True

    b. False

12. Which goaltender posted the best save percentage in a season with a minimum of 24 games played?

    a. Aaron Dell

    b. Alex Stalock

    c. Martin Jones

    d. Antti Niemi

13. How many faceoffs did the squad win in 2007-08?

   a. 2,076

   b. 2,179

   c. 1,789

   d. 1,878

14. The highest plus/minus rating recorded in a season as of 2020 is +31.

   a. True

   b. False

15. How many career shutouts did Evgeni Nabokov record with the Sharks?

   a. 42

   b. 47

   c. 50

   d. 53

16. How many points did Pat Falloon tally in the club's inaugural season?

   a. 39

   b. 46

   c. 38

   d. 59

17. Who recorded the most penalty minutes in a season?

   a. Link Gaetz

   b. Jeff Odgers

   c. Andrei Nazarov

   d. Doug Zmolek

18. Which Sharks goaltender has conceded the most goals in a regular season as of 2020?

    a. Martin Jones

    b. Jeff Hackett

    c. Evgeni Nabokov

    d. Artūrs Irbe

19. Which player has scored the most goals in one regular season?

    a. Jonathan Cheechoo

    b. Dany Heatley

    c. Joe Pavelski

    d. Owen Nolan

20. Joe Thornton averaged 1.70 points per game in 2005-06.

    a. True

    b. False

QUIZ ANSWERS

1. A – Joe Thornton

2. D – 21

3. B – False

4. D – 5

5. C – 75

6. D – 77

7. B – 2008-09

8. A – True

9. D – 4,561

10. C – 66

11. A – True

12. B – Alex Stalock

13. B – 2,179

14. A – True

15. C – 50

16. D – 59

17. A – Link Gaetz

18. D – Artūrs Irbe

19. A – Jonathan Cheechoo

20. B – False

DID YOU KNOW?

1. When the 2019-20 NHL regular season officially came to an end, the Sharks possessed an all-time (won-lost-tied-overtime/shootout losses) record of 1,049-892-121-156 for 2,375 points. The club was 119-122 in the playoffs and had made the postseason 21 times as of 2020.

2. The most points the Sharks have earned in a season was the 117 they posted in 2008-09 with a record of 53-18-11. The fewest points taken was 24, which came in 1992-93 with a mark of 11-71-2. Their best points percentage was .713 which also came in 2008-09 and the 1992-93 season was their lowest at just .143.

3. At the conclusion of the 2019-20 season, Patrick Marleau was the team's all-time leader with 1,551 games, 518 goals, and 1,102 points. Joe Thornton had collected the most assists with 804 and also owned the best plus/minus rating with +161. Sergei Makarov had the best career shooting percentage at 19.0% and Jonathan Cheechoo led with 9 hat tricks.

4. Patrick Marleau was also tops in even-strength goals (340), power-play goals (161), shorthanded markers (17), game-winning goals (101), and shots on net (3,899). When it comes to the career penalty leader for the franchise, Jeff Odgers was tops with 1.001 minutes, followed closely by Owen Nolan with 934.

5. On a career per-game basis for the Sharks, Evander Kane led the way with 0.42 regular-season goals per game at the end of 2019,-20 while Joe Thornton had earned 0.73 assists per contest and 0.96 points per outing. Meanwhile, Dany Heatley was tops in goals created per game at 0.35.

6. When it comes to season leaders, Jonathan Cheechoo scored the most goals (56), even-strength markers (30), power-play goals (24), and hat tricks (5) and shared the most game-winners with Joe Pavelski (11). Joe Thornton had the most assists (92) and points (114) and shared the best plus/minus rating (+31) with Marc-Edouard Vlasic. Jamie Baker and Jeff Friesen share the mark with 6 shorthanded tallies and Link Gaetz leads with 326 penalty minutes in a season. Brent Burns leads in shots on net (326) and Pavelski has the best shooting percentage (20.2%).

7. On a per-game basis during a single season, Jonathan Cheechoo scored at a 0.68 goals per game rate in 2005-06 while Joe Thornton notched 1.24 assists and 1.59 points-per-contest, also in 2005-06, and had a franchise-best goals created per game at 0.52.

8. In goaltending, the career regular-season leaders at the end of 2019-20 were Evgeni Nabokov in games played (563), wins (293), losses (178), ties/overtime/shootout losses (66), goals against (1,294), shots against (14,757), saves (13,463), shutouts (50) and minutes (32,492). Antti Niemi had the best save percentage (.917) while Vesa Toskala had the best goals-against average for a minimum of 100 games played (2.35)

9. On a seasonal goaltending basis, Evgeni Nabokov led the way in games played (77), wins (46), shots against (2,168), saves (1,998), shutouts (9), and minutes (4,561). Artūrs Irbe had the most ties/overtime/shootout losses (16) and goals against (209). Jeff Hackett and Steve Shields share the most losses (30) while Alex Stalock posted the best save percentage (.932) and goals-against average (1.87) in a minimum of 24 games played.

10. Where playoffs are concerned, Patrick Marleau played the most games (177), scored the most goals (68), game-winners (16), overtime goals (4), power-play goals (23), shorthanded goals (4), and points (120). Joe Thornton has the most assists (90) and Ryan Clowe the most penalty minutes (97). For goaltenders, Evgeni Nabokov played the most games (80) and had the best goals-against average (2.29) with a minimum of 20 games played, while Martin Jones had the best save percentage (.916) in a minimum 20 games.

CHAPTER 7:

THE TRADE MARKET

QUIZ TIME!

1. Which player was not traded to the Boston Bruins to acquire Joe Thornton?

    a. Wayne Primeau

    b. Brad Stuart

    c. Niko Dimitrakos

    d. Marco Sturm

2. In 1995, the Sharks traded Bob Errey to Detroit for a draft pick in which round?

    a. 7th

    b. 5th

    c. 6th

    d. 10th

3. On Feb. 24, 2020, the Sharks traded Patrick Marleau to Pittsburgh for a 3rd-round draft pick.

    a. True

    b. False

4. How many trades did the club make in 2002-03?

   a. 14
   b. 10
   c. 13
   d. 8

5. The Sharks acquired defenseman Dan Boyle from which team in 2008-09?

   a. Montreal Canadiens
   b. Florida Panthers
   c. Tampa Bay Lightning
   d. New York Rangers

6. In 1993-94, the Sharks traded Ulf Dahlén, Michal Sýkora, and Chris Terreri for which player?

   a. Todd Gill
   b. Marty McSorley
   c. Yves Racine
   d. Ed Belfour

7. What did the Sharks not send to the Minnesota Wild when trading for Brent Burns?

   a. 2011 1st-round pick
   b. Charlie Coyle
   c. 2011 4th-round pick
   d. Devin Setoguchi

8. The Sharks traded goalie Miikka Kiprusoff for a 1st-round draft pick in 2003-04.

   a. True
   b. False

9. Who was the first player San Jose acquired by trade in 1991-92?

   a. Tony Hrkac
   b. Doug Wilson
   c. Brian Mullen
   d. Wayne Presley

10. In 2019-20, the Sharks traded Barclay Goodrow to Tampa for which package?

    a. Brandon Davidson and a 2020 2nd-round pick
    b. Brandon Davidson, Anthony Greco, and a 2020 3rd-round pick
    c. A 2020 1st-round pick and Anthony Greco
    d. A 2020 1st and 2nd- round picks

11. The Sharks traded two players and two draft picks to Ottawa to acquire defender Erik Karlsson.

    a. True
    b. False

12. In 2002-03, San Jose traded which player for Alyn McCauley, Brad Boyes, and a 2003 1st-round pick?

    a. Brad Boyes
    b. Matt Bradley
    c. Owen Nolan
    d. Niklas Sundström

13. Which player did the Sharks swap for Igor Larionov in a trade with Detroit in 1995-96?

    a. Ben Hankinson
    b. Marc Bergevin

c. Dan McGillis

d. Ray Sheppard

14. San Jose made 13 trades in its inaugural season.

    a. True

    b. False

15. Which player did the Sharks not acquire by trade with Toronto in the 2015-16 season?

    a. Patrick McNally

    b. Roman Polák

    c. Nick Spaling

    d. James Reimer

16. Whom did the Sharks send to Buffalo with two draft picks for Evander Kane?

    a. Mirco Mueller

    b. Troy Grosenick

    c. Danny O'Regan

    d. Brandon Bollig

17. Which players were sent to Anaheim to acquire Teemu Selanne?

    a. Johan Hedberg and Jeff Friesen

    b. Jeff Friesen and Steve Shields

    c. Andy Sutton and Bobby Dolllas

    d. Steve Shields and Johan Hedberg

18. From which club did San Jose acquire Bill Guerin?

    a. New York Islanders

    b. Minnesota Wild

c. Boston Bruins

d. St. Louis Blues

19. The Sharks traded Mikael Samuelsson and Christian Gosselin for whom in 2001-02?

a. Rich Pilon

b. Jeff Hackett

c. Adam Graves

d. Jeff Norton

20. In 2007, the Sharks traded Josh Gorges and a 1st-round draft pick to Montreal for Craig Rivet and a 5th-round pick.

a. True

b. False

QUIZ ANSWERS

1. C – Niko Dimitrakos

2. B – 5th

3. A – True

4. A – 14

5. C – Tampa Bay Lightning

6. D – Ed Belfour

7. C – A 2011 4th-round pick

8. B – False

9. A – Tony Hrkac

10. C – 2020 1st-round pick and Anthony Greco

11. B – False

12. C – Owen Nolan

13. D – Ray Sheppard

14. A – True

15. A – Patrick McNally

16. C – Danny O'Regan

17. B – Jeff Friesen and Steve Shields

18. D – St. Louis Blues

19. C – Adam Graves

20. A – True

DID YOU KNOW?

1. In the first trade the Sharks made, they acquired Tony Hrkac from the Quebec Nordiques for fellow forward Greg Paslawski on May 30, 1991. Hrkac scored 12 points in 22 games before being traded to Chicago in February 1992. He won a Stanley Cup with Dallas in 1999 and retired with 371 points in 758 regular-season games. Paslawski, who was claimed by San Jose in the 1991 NHL expansion draft, finished his career with 372 points in 650 games.

2. Another trade, on May 30, 1991, sent Brian Mullen to San Jose from the New York Rangers for fellow forward Tim Kerr. Mullen notched 46 points in 72 games before being traded to the New York Islanders for the rights to Marcus Thuresson in August 1992. Mullen suffered a career-ending stroke a year later and retired with 622 points in 832 regular-season games. Kerr was taken by San Jose in the expansion draft and played another 54 games in New York before retiring with 370 goals and 674 points in 655 contests.

3. When the 1991 NHL expansion draft was held, San Jose agreed not to select forward Mike Craig from the Minnesota North Stars. In return, they received a second-round draft pick in 1991 and a first-rounder in 1992. These were used to select defender Sandis Ozolinsh and forward Andrei Nazarov, respectively. Ozolinsh scored 116 points

in 173 games before being traded to Colorado for Owen Nolan, while Nazarov registered 51 points in 169 outings before being dealt to Tampa in a multi-player trade in March 1998.

4. In November 2005, the Sharks picked up the former first overall draft pick Joe Thornton from Boston for fellow forwards Marco Sturm and Wayne Primeau along with defender Brad Stuart. Thornton, a four-time All-Star, became one of the Sharks' franchise leaders and captains with an Art Ross Trophy and a Hart Trophy to his name and is still playing. Stuart won the Stanley Cup with Detroit in 2008 before returning to San Jose for two seasons. He posted 335 points in 1,056 regular-season games. Sturm retired after notching 487 points in 938 outings while Primeau played 774 contests with 194 points.

5. Defender Marc-Edouard Vlasic joined San Jose from Calgary when the team picked up a second-round draft pick for goaltender Miikka Kiprusoff in November 2003. Vlasic was drafted 35th overall in 2005 and was still with the club in 2019-20. He had posted 326 points in 1,035 games with a +122 rating, adding 39 points and a +20 rating in 142 playoff matches. Kiprusoff made one All-Star Team and won the William M. Jennings and Vezina Trophies in 2006-06 and played 623 regular-season games with a record of 319-213-71.

6. Another huge deal for the Sharks was acquiring stud blue-liner Brent Burns and a second-round draft pick in June 2011 from Minnesota for forwards Devin Setoguchi and

Charlie Coyle and a 2011 first-round draft pick (Zack Phillips). Burns is still playing and is a three-time All-Star who won the Norris Trophy in 2016-17. Setoguchi finished his career with 261 points in 561 regular-season games while Coyle, who played with Boston in 2019-20, has scored 285 points in 570 games. Phillips has yet to play an NHL game.

7. The Sharks traded captain Owen Nolan to Toronto in March 2003 for fellow forwards Alyn McCauley and Brad Boyes, along with a first-round draft pick that was later dealt to Boston. Nolan was the face of the franchise at the time and posted 451 points in 568 games with San Jose, adding 27 points in 40 postseason outings. McCauley registered 83 points before signing with Los Angeles in 2006. He retired soon afterward due to concussions. Boyes played just one game for San Jose before being traded to Boston a year later for Jeff Jillson.

8. Future Hall-of-Fame netminder Ed Belfour showed up in San Jose in January 1997 when the Sharks sent Chris Terreri, Michal Sýkora, and Ulf Dahlen to Chicago. Belfour played well below par with the Sharks, though, compiling a 3-9 record in 13 games along with a .884 save percentage and a 3.41 goals-against average. Belfour signed as a free agent with Dallas six months later.

9. Doug Wilson, who has been the Sharks general manager since May 2003, was acquired in a trade with Chicago in September 1991 and became the team's first captain. He posted 48 points in 86 games before retiring. Going to

Chicago was fellow blue-liner Kerry Toporowski and a second-round draft choice. Toporowski was drafted 67th overall by the Sharks in 1991 but never made it to the NHL.

10. Former Sharks captain and all-time leading scorer Patrick Marleau left in 2017 to sign as a free agent with Toronto but was reacquired in October 2019 as a free agent. Marleau posted 10 goals and 20 points in 58 games before being dealt to Pittsburgh in February 2020 to give him a shot at winning the Stanley Cup. However, the Penguins were eliminated in the playoff qualifiers by Montreal in August 2020 in the COVID-19-affected season. San Jose picked up a 2021 third-round draft pick in the deal.

CHAPTER 8:

DRAFT DAY

QUIZ TIME!

1. Which player did the Sharks select 9th overall in the 2015 draft?

    a. Dylan Gambrell

    b. Kevin Labanc

    c. Timo Meier

    d. Nikolay Goldobin

2. In which round did the Sharks select Joe Pavelski in 2003?

    a. 5th

    b. 6th

    c. 7th

    d. 8th

3. Every player San Jose drafted in 2001 played at least one NHL game.

    a. True

    b. False

4. Who did the team draft 21st overall in 1996?

    a. Matt Bradley
    b. Marco Sturm
    c. Shean Donovan
    d. Scott Hannan

5. Which of these players was not selected 2nd overall by the Sharks?

    a. Pat Falloon
    b. Patrick Marleau
    c. Andrei Zyuzin
    d. Brad Stuart

6. How many players have the Sharks selected in the top 10 of the draft as of 2019?

    a. 9
    b. 11
    c. 8
    d. 10

7. Who did the team select 17th overall in 2012?

    a. Chris Tierney
    b. Mirco Mueller
    c. Matt Nieto
    d. Tomas Hertl

8. As of 2019, the Sharks have drafted 30 goalies.

    a. True
    b. False

9. As of 2019, what is the lowest number of players the Sharks have selected in a draft?

    a. 5
    b. 4
    c. 7
    d. 6

10. In 1994, the Sharks selected five players at which position?

    a. Right wing
    b. Defense
    c. Center
    d. Left wing

11. Pat Falloon was the franchise's first draft selection in 1991.

    a. True
    b. False

12. Who did the Sharks select 30th overall in 1991?

    a. Dale Craigwell
    b. Dody Wood
    c. Ray Whitney
    d. Sandis Ozolinsh

13. Which defenseman was drafted 35th overall in 2005?

    a. Matt Carle
    b. Jason Demers
    c. Marc-Edouard Vlasic
    d. Derek Joslin

14. The Sharks drafted goalies Miika Kiprusoff and Vesa Toskala in 1995.

    a. True
    b. False

15. Which of these goalies was not drafted by San Jose?

    a. Darcy Kuemper
    b. Alex Stalock
    c. Evgeni Nabokov
    d. Thomas Greiss

16. How many centers has the club drafted as of 2019?

    a. 44
    b. 53
    c. 46
    d. 50

17. Who was the only Sharks' draft choice in 2010 to play more than 100 NHL games?

    a. Sean Kuraly
    b. Charlie Coyle
    c. Matt Nieto
    d. Tommy Wingels

18. Of the 10 players the team drafted in 2004, how many were forwards?

    a. 8
    b. 1
    c. 3
    d. 5

19. Who was San Jose's 1st-round pick in 1994?

   a. Viktor Kozlov

   b. Teemu Riihijärvi

   c. Jeff Friesen

   d. Vaclav Varada

20. The most selections the franchise has made in a single draft is 14 as of 2019.

   a. True

   b. False

QUIZ ANSWERS

1. C – Timo Meier

2. C – 7th

3. A – True

4. B – Marco Sturm

5. D – Brad Stuart

6. B – 11

7. D – Tomáš Hertl

8. B – False

9. A – 5

10. A – Right wing

11. A – True

12. D – Sandis Ozolinsh

13. C – Marc-Edouard Vlasic

14. A – True

15. A – Darcy Kuemper

16. D – 50

17. B – Charlie Coyle

18. C – 3

19. C – Jeff Friesen

20. B – False

DID YOU KNOW?

1. After the 2019 NHL entry draft was completed, the Sharks had selected a total of 232 players since joining the league. They had never selected first overall but had chosen second overall on three occasions. The club has also had 11 top-10 picks in its history and selected several players in the supplemental draft, which was for American college players, between 1991 and 1994.

2. The Sharks were involved in the May 1991 NHL dispersal and expansion drafts to help fill their roster when joining the league. They chose from the Minnesota North Stars' pool of players in the dispersal draft and then from the rest of the NHL teams' pool of players in the expansion draft. The North Stars also chose players in the expansion draft to help re-stock their roster.

3. San Jose selected 24 total players from the Minnesota North Stars' unprotected list in the somewhat complicated dispersal draft. After these players were chosen, Minnesota and San Jose then took turns selecting unprotected players in the expansion draft with San Jose choosing another 10 players.

4. The most successful and most popular player taken in the 1991 dispersal draft from Minnesota was arguably goaltender Artūrs Irbe, who was something of a cult and playoff hero with Sharks' fans. He was originally drafted

in the 10th round with the 196th overall pick in 1989. Irbe played 183 games with San Jose and 568 regular-season contests in the NHL. He led the league in games played three times in his career and in saves and shots against once each.

5. The first player drafted by San Jose in the NHL entry draft was winger Pat Falloon, with the second overall pick. He scored 25 goals and 59 points as a 19-year-old rookie and posted 162 points in 258 regular-season games with the club. Falloon was then traded to Philadelphia in November 1995.

6. The Sharks had drafted 28 players in the first round of the entry draft as of 2019. Just two of the 28 failed to play an NHL game during their career. They were Teemu Riihijärvi (12th in 1995) and Mike Morris 27th in 2002). Ryan Merkley had yet to play a game as of 2019-20 but was drafted with the 21st overall pick as recently as 2018.

7. The lowest-drafted Sharks' skater to play in more than 50 NHL games was defender Douglas Murray, who was taken in the eighth round with the 241st pick in 1999. He chipped in with 59 points in 451 regular-season outings and had a +32 rating before being traded to Pittsburgh in March 2013. Murray finished his career with 64 points in 518 career games.

8. The team has never drafted a goaltender in the first round; the highest-drafted netminder was taken in the third round with the 55th overall pick in 1996. The Sharks took a

gamble on Terry Friesen from Swift Current of the Western Hockey League; however, he never played an NHL game.

9. The Sharks did hit the goaltending jackpot in 1994, though, when they selected Evgeni Nabokov. He was the lowest-drafted franchise goalie to hit the big time, as he was selected in the ninth round with the 219th overall pick. Nabokov still holds several club goaltending records and finished his career with a record of 353-227-86 and 59 shutouts. Nabokov was a former rookie of the year who left the team in 2011 as a free agent.

10. The most truculent player drafted by the Sharks would appear to be Andrei Nazarov, who was chosen 10th overall in 1992. The winger racked up 1,409 career penalty minutes in 571 contests. Nazarov earned 490 of those minutes in 169 games with San Jose before being traded to Tampa Bay in March 1998. Nazarov also contributed 124 points in his regular-season NHL career.

CHAPTER 9:

GOALTENDER TIDBITS

QUIZ TIME!

1. How many goalies did the Sharks use in their inaugural season?

    a. 4

    b. 6

    c. 3

    d. 5

2. Which goalie manned the net for the club's first playoff appearance?

    a. Wade Flaherty

    b. Jimmy Waite

    c. Artūrs Irbe

    d. Mike Vernon

3. Evgeni Nabokov was the fourth NHL goalie to score a regular-season goal with a shot on net.

    a. True

    b. False

4. How many wins did James Reimer record after being acquired midway through a season?

    a. 10

    b. 6

    c. 8

    d. 12

5. What was Evgeni Nabokov's save percentage in 2009-10?

    a. .919

    b. .918

    c. .922

    d. .921

6. Which goalie played 43 of 48 games in the shortened 2012-13 regular season?

    a. Thomas Greiss

    b. Troy Grosenick

    c. Antti Niemi

    d. Alex Stalock

7. How many goals did Miikka Kiprusoff concede in his final season with the Sharks?

    a. 56

    b. 67

    c. 53

    d. 65

8. Ed Belfour lost 11 games for the squad in 1996-97.

    a. True

    b. False

9. Who had a 2.59 goals-against average in 37 games in 2005-06?

   a. Vesa Toskala
   b. Evgeni Nabokov
   c. Nolan Schaefer
   d. Brian Boucher

10. Which netminder posted an .896 save percentage in 1997-98?

   a. Steve Shields
   b. Kelly Hrudey
   c. Chris Terreri
   d. Mike Vernon

11. In 2017-18, Martin Jones and Aaron Dell combined for 10 shutouts.

   a. True
   b. False

12. Which goalie lost 13 of his 24 games in 1995-96?

   a. Chris Terreri
   b. Geoff Sarjeant
   c. Wade Flaherty
   d. Artūrs Irbe

13. What was Thomas Greiss' goals-against average in 2011-12?

   a. 2.16
   b. 2.87
   c. 2.30
   d. 2.42

14. Thirty-two goalies have played at least one game for the Sharks as of the end of 2019-20.

    a. True
    b. False

15. How many saves did Steve Shields make in 1999-00?

    a. 1,664
    b. 1,101
    c. 1,238
    d. 1,011

16. In his first season with the team, how many wins did Martin Jones record?

    a. 35
    b. 37
    c. 30
    d. 36

17. Who was the club's starting goalie in the 1996-97 campaign?

    a. Jason Muzzatti
    b. Artūrs Irbe
    c. Mike Vernon
    d. Kelly Hrudey

18. Who posted a record of 12-6-3 in 2008-09?

    a. Alex Stalock
    b. Nolan Schaefer
    c. Dimitri Patzold
    d. Brian Boucher

19. How many goalies have the Sharks used between the 1999-2000 and 2019-20 seasons?

    a. 13
    b. 17
    c. 12
    d. 16

20. Antti Niemi had 100 penalty minutes while playing for San Jose.

    a. True
    b. False

QUIZ ANSWERS

1. D – 5

2. C – Artūrs Irbe

3. A – True

4. B – 6

5. C – .922

6. C – Antti Niemi

7. D – 65

8. B – False

9. A – Vesa Toskala

10. D – Mike Vernon

11. A – True

12. C – Wade Flaherty

13. C – 2.30

14. B – False

15. A – 1,664

16. B – 37

17. D – Kelly Hrudey

18. C – Brian Boucher

19. D – 16

20. B – False

DID YOU KNOW?

1. By the end of the 2019-20 season, the Sharks had used 28 different goaltenders since making their NHL debut. Two of these netminders played just one regular-season game with the club, while seven of them played in 10 or fewer.

2. The most goaltenders San Jose has used in one season was five, which happened the first year the team joined the NHL. Those who shared the netminding duties that campaign and the number of appearances they made were Jeff Hackett (42), Jarmo Myllys (27), Artūrs Irbe (13), Brian Hayward (7), and Wade Flaherty (3).

3. The youngest goalie to play in a Sharks' regular-season game was Thomas Greiss, who was 21 years old when he played against Anaheim on Jan. 13, 2008, in his NHL debut. The oldest netminders to play were Kelly Hrudey and Mike Vernon. Hrudey was 36 years old in the 1997-98 campaign, while Vernon was 36 in 1999-2000.

4. Thomas Greiss was drafted 94th overall by San Jose in 2004 and played with the club from 2007-08 to 2012-13. He appeared in just 44 regular-season outings with a record of 17-16-3 with a goals-against average of 2.52 and a .912 save percentage. Greiss, who was born in Germany, signed with Phoenix as a free agent in 2013 and went on to share the William M. Jennings Trophy with the New York Islanders in 2019-19.

5. The only former Sharks' goaltender to be inducted into the Hockey Hall of Fame is Ed Belfour. His time with the team was brief, though, as he was acquired in a January 1995 trade with Chicago. He then went 3-9 with the team before signing with Dallas as a free agent in July 1997. Belfour was a three-time All-Star who won the Calder Trophy as well as two Vezina Trophies and four Jennings Trophies and a Stanley Cup with Dallas in 1998-99.

6. Brian Boucher's stint with San Jose was also a short one after signing as a free agent in February 2008. He played just 27 regular-season games with the squad until signing as a free agent with Philadelphia. In those games, he went 15-7-4 with a .919 save percentage and a very healthy 2.12 goals-against average with three shutouts. The save percentage and goals-against average are club bests for goaltenders with at least 25 games played.

7. One of the finest goaltending seasons posted by a Shark was Alex Stalock's performance in 2013-14. He appeared in 24 contests with a mark of 12-5-2, a 1.87 goals-against average, and a .932 save percentage. He also got into three playoff games with a .929 save percentage and a 2.05 goals-against average. Stalock was traded to Toronto in February 2016 in a deal that saw fellow goaltender James Reimer arrive in San Jose.

8. When James Reimer got to San Jose near the end of the 2015-16 season, he basically stood on his head for the short time he was there. Reimer posted a mark of 6-2 with a .938 save percentage and a 1.62 goals-against average, recording

three shutouts. He appeared to be a fine choice as a backup to Martin Jones, but he signed as a free agent with Florida just five months after being traded to the Sharks.

9. Sharks goalies have never really been known as a rambunctious bunch, but Evgeni Nabokov did manage to reach 100 penalty minutes with the team in 563 regular-season games. However, he served just 6 minutes in 80 playoff outings. The only other Sharks' goalies to reach at least 30 penalty minutes were Steve Shields (37), Artūrs Irbe (34), and Mike Vernon (32).

10. Evgeni Nabokov was also the best stickhandler in San Jose's goaltending history, as he posted 10 points. He is also just one of eight NHL goalies to ever score a goal by shooting the puck in the opponent's net. Nabokov found the back of the net on March 10, 2002, against the Vancouver Canucks. In doing so, he became the first European netminder to score in the NHL and the first goalie to score a power-play marker.

CHAPTER 10:

ODDS & ENDS

QUIZ TIME!

1. How many regular-season games have the Sharks tied in their history?

    a. 139

    b. 120

    c. 121

    d. 135

2. Who was assessed the team's first-ever penalty?

    a. Rob Zettler

    b. Mike McHugh

    c. Link Gaetz

    d. Wayne Presley

3. Whenever the Sharks are awarded a power play at home, the theme from *Jaws* is played at the rink.

    a. True

    b. False

4. Who was the first to record a hat trick in a regular-season game?

    a. Johan Garpenlöv
    b. Igor Larionov
    c. Rob Gaudreau
    d. Ulf Dahlen

5. Who is the club's mascot?

    a. Sherman the Shark
    b. Bill Shark
    c. Chomper
    d. S.J. Sharkie

6. As of 2020, which player's goal song is *Radio Gaga* by Queen?

    a. Brent Burns
    b. Logan Couture
    c. Joe Thornton
    d. Timo Meier

7. Who were the Shark's television commentators for the team's first three years?

    a. Joe Starkey and Chris Collins
    b. Joe Starkey and Pete Stemkowski
    c. Randy Hahn and Chris Collins
    d. Randy Hahn and Pete Stemkowski

8. In 2015-16, the Sharks finished in 6th place in the Western Conference.

    a. True
    b. False

9. How many times has San Jose finished in last place in their division, as of 2020?

    a. 6
    b. 4
    c. 8
    d. 5

10. Which player holds the franchise record for most penalty minutes in a single game with 41?

    a. Doug Zmolek
    b. Jeff Odgers
    c. Jody Shelley
    d. Link Gaetz

11. As of 2019, 337 skaters have played in at least one game for the Sharks.

    a. True
    b. False

12. How many players have scored 4 or more goals in a game as of 2020?

    a. 5
    b. 3
    c. 6
    d. 4

13. When did the Sharks host their first All-Star Game?

    a. 1995
    b. 1996
    c. 1997
    d. 1998

14. The first-ever penalty received by a Sharks player was for holding.

    a. True
    b. False

15. How many regular-season games has Patrick Marleau played for the Sharks, as of 2020?

    a. 1,551
    b. 1,543
    c. 1,558
    d. 1,560

16. What is the Sharks' longest regular-season winning streak?

    a. 11
    b. 12
    c. 17
    d. 15

17. During the team's home game introductions, what do the players skate through onto the ice?

    a. Fishnet
    b. A boat
    c. Fake aquarium
    d. A shark head

18. What is the most goals the club has scored in a regular season as of 2020?

    a. 256
    b. 254
    c. 265
    d. 248

19. Who scored the club's first regular-season penalty shot?

    a. Jeff Friesen

    b. Sergei Makarov

    c. Kevin Miller

    d. Alexander Korolyuk

20. Ulf Dahlen scored the first playoff hat trick for the Sharks on May 6, 1994.

    a. True

    b. False

QUIZ ANSWERS

1. C – 121

2. D – Wayne Presley

3. A – True

4. C – Rob Gaudreau

5. D – S.J. Sharkie

6. C – Joe Thornton

7. B – Joe Starkey and Pete Stemkowski

8. A – True

9. A – 6

10. C – Jody Shelley

11. B – False

12. D – 4

13. C – 1997

14. B – False

15. A – 1,551

16. A – 11

17. D – A shark head

18. C – 265

19. B – Sergei Makarov

20. A – True

DID YOU KNOW?

1. The Sharks have had 10 different head coaches in their history. George Kingston was the first. He was followed by Kevin Constantine, Jim Wiley, Al Sims, Darryl Sutter, Cap Raeder, Ron Wilson, Todd McLellan, Peter DeBoer, and current head coach Bob Boughner, who was hired on Dec. 11, 2019.

2. The shortest San Jose head coaching stint belongs to Cap Raeder who took over the club for just one game in 2003 after Darryl Sutter left and before Ron Wilson was hired. The longest stint was by Todd McLellan, who coached 540 regular-season games between June 11, 2008, and April 20, 2015. He also coached the most playoff contests, 62.

3. Todd McLellan currently holds Sharks' regular-season coaching records for wins (311), overtime/shootout losses (66), points (688), and points percentage (.637). Darryl Sutter has the most losses (167) and ties (60). Peter DeBoer has the most playoff wins (32), while McLellan has the most playoff defeats (32). The best winning percentage in the playoffs belongs to Ron Wilson (.538).

4. There have been just four general managers in Sharks' history as of mid-2020. Jack Ferreira was the first, followed by Chuck Grillo, Dean Lombardi, and the current GM, Doug Wilson, who took over the job on May 13, 2003. Lombardi is the son-in-law of Hockey Hall of Famer Bob Pulford.

5. Jack Ferreira, Chuck Grillo, and Dean Lombardi were all formerly employed by the Minnesota North Stars and joined the Sharks when San Jose was awarded an NHL franchise. Grillo was originally the Sharks' vice-president of player personnel and was also named executive vice-president of the club in 1995 until 1996, when Lombardi was hired as GM.

6. When Dean Lombardi became general manager of the club in 1996, the team's point total increased for six consecutive seasons. This feat had been achieved just once before by a general manager in the annals of the NHL, when Hall of Famer Bill Torrey's New York Islanders increased their point totals for seven straight seasons in the early 1970s.

7. Current general manager Doug Wilson has been the longest-serving and most successful general manager of the Sharks. Since May 2003, he has helped the franchise win a Presidents' Trophy, a conference title, and five division titles. His teams have made the playoffs 14 times as of 2019-20 and reached the Stanley Cup final in 2015-16.

8. The Sharks' famous mascot was introduced to home fans on Jan. 28, 1992. The unnamed mascot was introduced between periods of a contest with the New York Rangers and a contest was then held to give the mascot a name. The winning name, "S. J. Sharkie" was announced about 10 weeks later, when all votes were tallied.

9. Sharks' enforcer Link Gaetz was known as "The Missing Link," which is one of the greatest nicknames in sports

history. The defender was claimed from Minnesota in the 1991 NHL dispersal draft and played 48 games in the team's first season. He racked up a club record 326 penalty minutes for an average of 6.79 minutes per game. Gaetz didn't play the next season due to an auto accident, was traded to Edmonton in September 1993, and spent the rest of his career in the minors.

10. NHL history was made on March 10, 1995, when the league had to cancel a game due to rain. This occurred when the banks of the Guadalupe River flooded and made it impossible for fans to reach the San Jose Arena for a contest between San Jose and the Detroit Red Wings. The game was played on April 5, with Detroit winning 5-3.

CHAPTER 11:

KINGS ON THE BLUE LINE

QUIZ TIME!

1. Which defenseman earned 25 assists in the club's first season?

    a. David Williams

    b. Neil Wilkinson

    c. Doug Wilson

    d. Jay More

2. How many points did Gary Suter tally in 2001-02?

    a. 32

    b. 28

    c. 40

    d. 33

3. Defenseman Marc-Edouard Vlasic had the lowest plus/minus rating on the team in 2014-15 at -15.

    a. True

    b. False

4. How many points did Brent Burns compile to lead the Sharks in 2017-18?

   a. 63
   b. 66
   c. 67
   d. 70

5. Who scored 5 game-winning goals in 1998-99?

   a. Mike Rathje
   b. Jeff Norton
   c. Bill Houlder
   d. Andrei Zyuzin

6. How many defensemen suited up for the Sharks in their inaugural season?

   a. 10
   b. 14
   c. 9
   d. 12

7. What was Mike Rathje's team-low plus/minus rating in 2002-03?

   a. -15
   b. -19
   c. -24
   d. -20

8. Doug Zmolek was the only defenseman to play all 84 games in 1992-93.

   a. True
   b. False

9. How many goals did Sandis Ozolinsh score in 1993-94?

   a. 9

   b. 26

   c. 7

   d. 15

10. Which defenseman notched 42 points in 2006-07?

   a. Marc-Edouard Vlasic

   b. Scott Hannan

   c. Christian Ehrhoff

   d. Matt Carle

11. In 2008-09, four Sharks defenders blocked over 100 shots apiece.

   a. True

   b. False

12. How many penalty minutes did Marty McSorley receive in 1997-98?

   a. 177

   b. 186

   c. 140

   d. 144

13. Who was the only defender to register over 100 blocked shots and 100 hits in 2018-19?

   a. Justin Braun

   b. Tim Heed

   c. Radim Šimek

   d. Brent Burns

14. Sharks' rearguards combined for 30 points in their 2003-04 playoff run.

    a. True
    b. False

15. Who posted 43 points in 2005-06?

    a. Josh Gorges
    b. Rob Davison
    c. Scott Preissing
    d. Kyle McLaren

16. Which defenseman had a plus/minus rating of +19 in 2010-11?

    a. Ian White
    b. Kent Huskins
    c. Dan Boyle
    d. Jason Demers

17. How many shots on net did Brent Burns register in the 2015-16 season?

    a. 224
    b. 353
    c. 268
    d. 347

18. Who led the Sharks' blue line in assists with 13 in the shortened 48-game 2012-13 season?

    a. Douglas Murray
    b. Brad Stuart
    c. Dan Boyle
    d. Justin Braun

19. This defenseman scored 3 game-winning goals in 2001-02.

   a. Marcus Ragnarsson

   b. Brad Stuart

   c. Bryan Marchment

   d. Mike Rathje

20. Brendan Dillon had 127 hits in only 60 games played in 2014-15.

   a. True

   b. False

QUIZ ANSWERS

1. A – David Williams

2. D – 33

3. B – False

4. C – 67

5. C – Bill Houlder

6. D – 12

7. B – -19

8. A – True

9. B – 26

10. D – Matt Carle

11. B – False

12. C – 140

13. A – Justin Braun

14. B – False

15. C – Scott Preissing

16. D – Jason Demers

17. B – 353

18. C – Dan Boyle

19. A – Marcus Ragnarsson

20. A – True

DID YOU KNOW?

1. Two former Sharks defenders have been inducted into the Hockey Hall of Fame in Toronto. Rob Blake, who is currently the general manager of the Los Angeles Kings, received the honor in 2014 while current Sharks' general manager Doug Wilson was a member of the 2020 inductee class.

2. Doug Wilson was acquired by San Jose via a trade with Chicago just before the team's debut season and was the Sharks' first captain. He won the Norris Trophy in 1981-82 and was a First Team All-Star in 1981–82 and a Second-Team All-Star in 1984–85 and 1989–90. He's the career leader for the Chicago Blackhawks in goals and points by a defenseman. Wilson was Chicago's top-scoring blue-liner for 10 straight seasons and finished his career with 827 points in 1,024 games, with 80 points in 95 playoff outings.

3. Rob Blake joined San Jose as a free agent in 2008 and signed for another season in 2009-10, when he served as team captain. He tallied 75 points in 143 games with the club and notched 777 points in 1,270 regular-season games during his NHL career. Blake, who also played with Los Angeles and Colorado, retired in 2010. He was a four-time All-Star and a member of the All-Rookie Team in 1990-1991. Blake won the James Norris Trophy in 1997-98 and a Stanley Cup with Colorado in 2000-01.

4. The highest-scoring defenseman in Sharks' history has been Brent Burns. At the conclusion of 2019-20, he had accumulated 155 goals, 356 assists, and 511 points in 660 regular-season games, adding 20 goals and 59 points in 83 playoff matches. Burns also led defenders with 48 career regular-season power-play goals and 26 game-winners.

5. High-scoring rearguard Erik Karlsson joined San Jose in a big September 2018 trade from Ottawa where he was team captain and four-time All-Star and had won the James Norris Trophy twice. At the end of 2019-20, Karlsson had registered 85 points in 109 games with the Sharks and 16 points in 19 playoff outings. In June 2019, he signed an eight-year, $92 million deal to become the highest-paid blue-liner in NHL history.

6. Bryan Marchment, who played 334 regular-season games with San Jose, is currently ranked first in penalty minutes for a Sharks' defenseman with 706. This third in club history. Marchment also chipped in with 66 points and a +33 rating in his stint from 1998 to 2003. He served 2,307 minutes in his 926-game NHL career with another 102 minutes in 83 playoff encounters.

7. At the conclusion of 2019-20, Marc-Edouard Vlasic had posted the highest career +minus on the team for a blue-liner at +122. This was second on the club to Joe Thornton's +161. In addition, Vlasic had played the third-most regular-season games in Sharks' history at 1,035 and had contributed 72 goals and 326 points.

8. One of the Sharks' most underrated rearguards was the undrafted Dan Boyle, who was acquired in a trade with Tampa in July 2008. Boyle was a two-time All-Star who notched 269 points in 431 regular-season games with San Jose, compiled a +19 rating, and had 48 points in 68 playoff games. He was traded to the New York Islanders in June 2014 and finished his career with 605 points in 1,093 outings, with 81 points in 130 playoff contests. Boyle also won a Stanley Cup with Tampa in 2003-04.

9. Former 1985-86 NHL Rookie of the Year Gary Suter played the final 227 contests of his 1,145-game career with the Sharks. He was acquired from Chicago in June 1998 for a ninth-round draft choice. Suter played just one game in his first campaign due to injury, then chipped in with 101 points and a +28 rating. He finished his career with an All-Star nod, a Stanley Cup with Calgary in 1988-89, and 844 points with a +126 rating. He also added 73 points in 108 playoff clashes.

10. One of the longest-serving blue-liners was Mike Rathje, who was drafted third overall by San Jose in 1992. He skated in 671 regular-season games, tallying 155 points and a +11 rating. Rathje cracked the lineup as a teenager and played 11 seasons before signing with Philadelphia as a free agent in August 2005. He also notched 23 points in 73 playoff contests with the Sharks.

CHAPTER 12:

CENTERS OF ATTENTION

QUIZ TIME!

1. How many points did Todd Elik post in 1994-95?

   a. 22

   b. 17

   c. 25

   d. 16

2. Which center led the Sharks with 218 hits in the 2013-14 campaign?

   a. Logan Couture

   b. Andrew Desjardins

   c. Tommy Wingels

   d. Joe Thornton

3. Jamie Baker notched 18 points in the 1993-94 playoffs for the Sharks.

   a. True

   b. False

4. Which center had a faceoff win percentage of 60.2% in 2009-10?

   a. Scott Nichol

   b. Joe Thornton

   c. Joe Pavelski

   d. Manny Malhotra

5. What was Mike Sullivan's plus/minus rating in 1992-93?

   a. -42

   b. +2

   c. -50

   d. +4

6. Which center scored 12 goals in the 2005-06 season?

   a. Marcel Goc

   b. Mark Smith

   c. Grant Stevenson

   d. Alyn McCauley

7. How many power-play goals did Joe Pavelski score in 2018-19?

   a. 10

   b. 7

   c. 12

   d. 14

8. Vincent Damphousse posted an impressive 37 assists in only 45 games in 2000-01.

   a. True

   b. False

9. Who scored 10 game-winning goals in 2007-08?

    a. Marcel Goc

    b. Torrey Mitchell

    c. Patrick Marleau

    d. Jeremy Roenick

10. How many goals did Logan Couture tally in 2017-18?

    a. 17

    b. 26

    c. 34

    d. 22

11. Six of San Jose's centers played all 48 games in the 2012-13 season.

    a. True

    b. False

12. Which center lost 468 faceoffs in 2017-18?

    a. Danny O'Regan

    b. Ryan Carpenter

    c. Tomas Hertl

    d. Chris Tierney

13. Who registered 14 goals in the 2015-16 playoffs?

    a. Logan Couture

    b. Joe Pavelski

    c. Joe Thornton

    d. Patrick Marleau

14. Tomas Hertl contributed 4 shorthanded goals in 2018-19.

    a. True
    b. False

15. How many goals did Mike Ricci score in the 2002-03 season?

    a. 10
    b. 7
    c. 19
    d. 11

16. What was Logan Couture's team-high plus/minus rating in 2012-13?

    a. +7
    b. +10
    c. +9
    d. +15

17. Which center scored 3 shorthanded goals in the club's inaugural season?

    a. Perry Berezan
    b. Mike Sullivan
    c. Kelly Kisio
    d. Dean Evason

18. How many goals did Joe Thornton score in the 2007-08 season?

    a. 20
    b. 25
    c. 22
    d. 29

19. Which center earned 38 assists in 1993-94?

    a. Jamie Baker
    b. Jeff McLean
    c. Todd Elik
    d. Igor Larionov

20. Jeremy Roenick registered 24 penalty minutes in the 2008-09 season.

    a. True
    b. False

QUIZ ANSWERS

1. B – 17

2. C – Tommy Wingels

3. B – False

4. A – Scott Nichol

5. A – -42

6. D – Alyn McCauley

7. C – 12

8. A – True

9. D – Jeremy Roenick

10. C – 34

11. B – False

12. D – Chris Tierney

13. B – Joe Pavelski

14. B – False

15. D – 11

16. A – +7

17. C – Kelly Kisio

18. D – 29

19. D – Igor Larionov

20. A – True

DID YOU KNOW?

1. Igor Larionov is the only former Sharks center in the Hockey Hall of Fame. He was drafted 214th overall by Vancouver in 1985 and joined the team four years later, when Russian-born players were allowed to leave to play in the NHL. Larionov was claimed on waivers by San Jose in October 1992. He notched 82 points in 97 games with the Sharks and added 27 points in 25 playoff outings. Larionov was traded to Detroit in October 1995 and finished his career with 644 points in 921 games, with 97 points in 150 playoff outings.

2. Former center Vincent Damphousse enjoyed an excellent NHL career, tallying 1,205 points in 1,378 games and 104 points in 140 playoff contests. He won a Stanley Cup with Montreal but is not yet in the Hall of Fame. The Sharks acquired him in March 1999 in a trade with Montreal and he played 385 games with the team while tallying 289 points and adding 38 points in 53 playoff encounters. Damphousse retired as a Shark in 2004.

3. Another high-scoring former Shark who hasn't made it to the Hall of Fame yet is Bernie Nicholls. He joined the team for the last 135 games of his career after signing as a free agent in August 1996 and he retired in 1999 at the age of 36. Nicholls, who once scored 70 goals and 80 assists in a season with Los Angeles, registered 475 goals and 1,209

points in 1,127 games, and added 114 points in 118 postseason games. He tallied 75 of those regular-season points with San Jose.

4. One more former Shark who could end up in the Hall of Fame, Jeremy Roenick, played the last two of his 20 NHL seasons with the team after signing as a free agent in 2007. He posted 46 points in 111 games as a checking center with 10 of his 14 markers in 2007-08 being game-winners. Roenick scored 513 goals and 1,216 points in 1,363 games and had 122 points in 154 playoff outings He scored his 500th goal, 700th assist, and 1,200th point while with San Jose.

5. One of the more recent centers with the club is Tomas Hertl, who joined the squad in 2013-14 after being drafted 17th overall in 2012. The alternate captain was just 26 years old when the 2019-20 season ended and had racked up 280 points in 453 games, along with 42 points in 62 postseason matches. Hertl became the first player born in the Czech Republic after the dissolution of Czechoslovakia to play in an NHL contest.

6. Joe Pavelski proved he could elevate his game in the playoffs as he scored a league-high 14 goals and added 9 assists for 23 points in 24 games in the 2015-16 postseason. He also led the league with 9 even-strength markers, 5 on the power play, and 4 game-winners. Pavelski competed in 134 playoff games with the team between 2007 and 2019 and totaled 48 goals and 52 assists for an even 100 points.

7. One of the Sharks' first centers was Kelly Kisio, who played in the club's first two NHL campaigns. Kisio was in his 10th season when San Jose debuted in 1991 after he had been acquired in a trade with the Minnesota North Stars. The veteran posted 37 points in 48 games his first year and then led the team in goals (26), assists (52), and points (78) in 78 games in 1992-93 before leaving at the end of the season to sign with Calgary.

8. Center Brian Lawton was drafted first overall by the Minnesota North Stars in the 1983 NHL entry draft, becoming the first American-born hockey player to be taken that high. He was also the first player to be drafted first overall from an American high school team. Lawton joined San Jose in August 1991 as a free agent and was traded to New Jersey in January 1993. In between, he tallied 47 points in 80 games for the team.

9. Mark Pavelich was a member of the famous "Miracle on Ice" 1980 U.S. Olympic hockey team that won a gold medal. He wasn't drafted into the NHL but signed with the New York Rangers and set a club record for points by a rookie with 76 in 1981-82. A year later, he became the first American to score 5 goals in an NHL game. Pavelich left the NHL to play in Europe in 1987 but returned to join the Sharks in their debut season. He played just two games and assisted on the team's first-ever goal by Craig Coxe and promptly retired.

10. With six Sutter brothers playing in the NHL, there was a good chance one of them would skate with the Sharks.

Ron Sutter joined the club as a free agent in October 1996 and notched just 15 goals and 41 points in 272 games playing as a defensive center for head coach and brother Darryl Sutter. He signed with Calgary in February 2001, played 21 more games, and then retired at the age of 37. Sutter played 19 NHL seasons and posted 535 points in 1,093 regular-season outings.

CHAPTER 13:

THE WINGERS TAKE FLIGHT

QUIZ TIME!

1. Who scored 10 power-play goals in the Sharks' inaugural season?

   a. Brian Lawton
   b. David Bruce
   c. Pat Falloon
   d. Brian Mullen

2. How many assists did Joonas Donskoi earn in 2015-16?

   a. 31
   b. 19
   c. 25
   d. 22

3. Brent Burns started his career playing on the wing before becoming a defenseman.

   a. True
   b. False

4. Which player registered 172 hits in 2018-19?

   a. Marcus Sorensen

   b. Timo Meier

   c. Barclay Goodrow

   d. Evander Kane

5. How many goals did Owen Nolan score in 1996-97?

   a. 15

   b. 12

   c. 44

   d. 31

6. Which winger recorded 48 points in 2002-03?

   a. Adam Graves

   b. Jonathan Cheechoo

   c. Marco Sturm

   d. Scott Thornton

7. Which winger blocked 45 shots in 2013-14?

   a. Matt Nieto

   b. James Sheppard

   c. Martin Havlát

   d. Mike Brown

8. Jamal Mayers led the Sharks with 124 penalty minutes in 2010-11.

   a. True

   b. False

9. How many assists did Jeff Friesen post in the 1999-2000 season?

    a. 28
    b. 35
    c. 40
    d. 25

10. Joel Ward notched how many points in the 2015-16 playoffs?

    a. 8
    b. 6
    c. 15
    d. 13

11. Winger Brad Winchester took 33 faceoffs in 2011-12.

    a. True
    b. False

12. How many points did Jonathan Cheechoo put up in 2005-06?

    a. 69
    b. 37
    c. 93
    d. 47

13. Who led the club with 25 goals in 1998-99?

    a. Alexander Korolyuk
    b. Joe Murphy
    c. Dave Lowry
    d. Ron Stern

14. Teemu Selanne scored 13 points in his first 12 games with the Sharks.

    a. True
    b. False

15. Who accumulated 79 penalty minutes in 28 games in 2012-13?

    a. T.J. Galiardi
    b. Tim Kennedy
    c. Martin Havlát
    d. Ryane Clowe

16. Which winger ended the 2006-07 season with 3 shorthanded goals?

    a. Mark bell
    b. Steve Bernier
    c. Mike Grier
    d. Milan Michálek

17. Who was the only winger to play all 82 games in 1996-97?

    a. Tony Granato
    b. Andrei Nazarov
    c. Shean Donovan
    d. Jeff Friesen

18. Who recorded 39 assists in 2000-01?

    a. Niklas Sundström
    b. Owen Nolan
    c. Stephane Matteau
    d. Tony Granato

19. Which winger scored 64 points in 2010-11?

   a. Ryane Clowe

   b. Dany Heatley

   c. Devin Setoguchi

   d. Ben Eager

20. Ron Stern posted the team's lowest plus/minus rating in 1999-00 with a -15.

   a. True

   b. False

QUIZ ANSWERS

1. B – David Bruce

2. C – 25

3. A – True

4. D – Evander Kane

5. D – 31

6. C – Marco Sturm

7. A – Matt Nieto

8. A – True

9. B – 35

10. D – 13

11. A – True

12. C – 93

13. B – Joe Murphy

14. A – True

15. D – Ryane Clowe

16. C – Mike Grier

17. D – Jeff Friesen

18. A – Niklas Sundström

19. B – Dany Heatley

20. B – False

DID YOU KNOW?

1. Two former Sharks wingers are enshrined in the Hockey Hall of Fame, as of 2020. Sergei Makarov was inducted in 2016 and Teemu Selanne was enshrined in 2017. Makarov was also inducted into the International Ice Hockey Federation (IIHF) Hall of Fame in 2001. As of 2020, Selanne was the highest-scoring player in Olympic hockey history with 43 points.

2. Teemu Selanne joined the Sharks in March 2001 via a trade with Anaheim. He posted 134 points in 176 games, led the team in goals with 29 in 2001-02, shared the lead in goals in 2002-03 with 28, and led the team with 64 points. He then joined Colorado as a free agent in 2003. Selanne set several NHL records and milestones during his career, was a four-time All-Star, and won Calder, Masterton, and Rocket Richard Trophies as well as a Stanley Cup in 2006-07 with Anaheim. He posted 684 goals and 1,457 points in 1,451 games, along with 88 points in 130 playoff contests and he led the league in goals three times.

3. Sergei Makarov posted 384 points in 424 career NHL games, adding 23 points in 34 playoff contests. However, he was inducted into the Hall of Fame mainly for his performances in the Soviet Union and while playing internationally. Calgary traded him to the Hartford Whalers on June 20, 1993, and San Jose acquired the 35-year-old from Hartford six days later in a deal that

involved swapping first-round draft picks. Ultimately, the Sharks gave up the second overall pick in 1993, which was used to select Hall-of-Fame blue-liner Chris Pronger.

4. Joe is definitely the most famous Thornton to play for the Sharks, but his cousin Scott Thornton also skated with the team from 2000 to 2006. The winger was originally drafted third overall by Toronto in 1989 and joined San Jose as a free agent. He notched 147 points in 342 games with the team before signing with Los Angeles.

5. Winger Dody Wood was drafted by San Jose 45th overall in 1991 for his toughness rather than scoring touch. He played 106 games with the club from 1992-93 to 1997-98 and was assessed 471 penalty minutes while chipping in with 18 points. Wood averaged 4.44 penalty minutes per game and was traded to New Jersey in December 1997. However, he never played another NHL game.

6. Just over 21% of Marco Sturm's 128 goals with the Sharks were game-winners. He scored 27 of them in his 553-game stint with the team from 1997-98 to 2005-06. This ranks him sixth all-time in that category in team history. Sturm was traded to Boston in November 2005 in the deal that brought Joe Thornton to San Jose. He finished his career with 242 goals and 43 game-winners.

7. Jonathan Cheechoo enjoyed a career year in 2005-06 with a San Jose record and league-high 56 goals, 93 points, and a league-best 11 game-winners. He tallied 28 goals the previous season and followed up with campaigns of 37 and 23 goals before tailing off with just 12 in 66 games in

2008-09. He was then traded to Ottawa in September 2009 and notched just five goals in 61 games with the Senators. Ottawa eventually bought out his contract and he never played another NHL game.

8. Winger Ray Whitney and his brother Dean were stick boys for Wayne Gretzky and the Edmonton Oilers when they were youngsters. Ray went on to become the second player ever drafted by the Sharks when he was selected 23rd overall in 1991. Whitney became one of the top scorers from that draft, posting 1,064 points in 1,330 regular-season games. He gathered 121 of those points in 200 games with San Jose before signing with Edmonton in 1997.

9. Rob Gaudreau was claimed by San Jose from Minnesota in the 1991 NHL dispersal draft and tallied 78 points in 143 games before being claimed by Ottawa in the 1995 waiver draft. Gaudreau scored the first two hat tricks in Sharks' history in 1992–93 and was the first Shark to be named the NHL's Rookie of the Month. He left the NHL in 1996 to play in Europe and retired just a year later at the age of 27.

10. Jeff Friesen was something of a special-teams master with the Sharks during his stint on the wing from 1994 to 2000 after being drafted 11th overall in 1994. He posted 149 goals and 350 points in 512 regular-season games with 43 goals and 109 points coming on the power play. He also scored 13 shorthanded goals and points. As of 2020, he was eighth on the team's career list in power-play markers and game-winners and fourth in shorthanded goals.

CHAPTER 14:

THE HEATED RIVALRIES

QUIZ TIME!

1. With which team did the Sharks engage in two brawls during a pre-season game in 2019-20?

    a. Chicago Blackhawks
    b. Calgary Flames
    c. Vegas Golden Knights
    d. Anaheim Ducks

2. Which team scored 15 goals against the Sharks in 6 regular-season games in 1993-94?

    a. Phoenix Coyotes
    b. Dallas Stars
    c. Los Angeles Kings
    d. Mighty Ducks of Anaheim

3. As of 2020, the Sharks and Los Angeles Kings have faced off in the playoffs five times.

    a. True
    b. False

4. Which team did the Sharks face in their first-ever playoff series in 1992-93?

    a. Detroit Red Wings
    b. Toronto Maple Leafs
    c. Vancouver Canucks
    d. Calgary Flames

5. Which club did the Sharks not defeat in the 2015-16 playoffs to reach the Stanley Cup final?

    a. Nashville Predators
    b. Los Angeles Kings
    c. Minnesota Wild
    d. St. Louis Blues

6. How many regular-season wins did San Jose have against the Winnipeg Jets through 35 meetings?

    a. 17
    b. 22
    c. 14
    d. 21

7. Which Vegas Golden Knights player did Evander Kane form a rivalry with following the teams' 2018-19 playoff series?

    a. Ryan Reaves
    b. Alex Tuch
    c. Ryan McNabb
    d. Cody Eakin

8. The Sharks beat the Vegas Golden Knights in their first playoff meeting in 2017-18.

   a. True
   b. False

9. The Calgary Flames scored how many goals against San Jose in the 1992-93 season?

   a. 27
   b. 42
   c. 52
   d. 26

10. How many goals did the Sharks tally against Chicago in the 2000-01 campaign?

    a. 17
    b. 11
    c. 15
    d. 12

11. As of 2020, San Jose hadn't won 100 regular-season games against any opponent.

    a. True
    b. False

12. How many regular-season contests did the Sharks win in their first 157 clashes with Los Angeles?

    a. 73
    b. 90
    c. 77
    d. 82

13. With how many teams did the Sharks not lose or tie a regulation game in the 2003-04 season?

    a. 6

    b. 4

    c. 5

    d. 3

14. The team with which San Jose has played the most ties was the Edmonton Oilers with 12.

    a. True

    b. False

15. The Sharks did not record at least 4 points against which team in the 2011-12 regular season?

    a. Boston Bruins

    b. Tampa Bay Lightning

    c. Edmonton Oilers

    d. Washington Capitals

16. How many regular-season games did the club lose to the Calgary Flames in 1992-93?

    a. 9

    b. 3

    c. 2

    d. 8

17. How many goals did San Jose tally against Pittsburgh in the 2015-16 Stanley Cup final?

    a. 15

    b. 12

c. 14

d. 13

18. Against which team have the Sharks not registered 400 regular-season goals, as of 2020?

a. Los Angeles Kings

b. Arizona Coyotes

c. Vancouver Canucks

d. Anaheim Ducks

19. How many teams did the Sharks fail to beat in their inaugural season?

a. 7

b. 8

c. 9

d. 10

20. The Sharks won all six matchups against Anaheim in the 1993-94 campaign.

a. True

b. False

QUIZ ANSWERS

1. C – Vegas Golden Knights

2. B – Dallas Stars

3. B – False

4. A – Detroit Red Wings

5. C – Minnesota Wild

6. D – 21

7. A – Ryan Reaves

8. B – False

9. C – 52

10. A – 17

11. A – True

12. D – 82

13. C – 5

14. A – True

15. B – Tampa Bay Lightning

16. D – 8

17. B – 12

18. C – Vancouver Canucks

19. C – 9

20. A – True

DID YOU KNOW?

1. When the Sharks entered the NHL in 1991-92 as the only expansion franchise, there were no natural rivals at the time other than the other California-based team, the Los Angeles Kings. However, a rivalry was soon formed when the nearby Anaheim Ducks joined the league in 1993 and another was added when the Vegas Golden Knights made their debut in 2017.

2. At the conclusion of the 2019-20 campaign, the Sharks' all-time regular-season (won-loss-tied-overtime/shootout) record against the Los Angeles Kings was 82-57-7-11. Against Anaheim, it was 74-55-4-10 and their mark against Vegas was 4-7-0-1.

3. The Sharks held a 3-0 series stranglehold lead over Los Angeles in the 2013-14 Western Conference quarterfinals but ended up losing the set in seven games. It was just the fourth time in NHL history that a 3-0 series lead was blown.

4. San Jose finished the 2008-09 season as the top team in the NHL with a record of 53-18-11 for 117 points. However, they were upset by Anaheim in the first round of the playoffs in six games when the Ducks entered the postseason as the eighth-seeded team in the Western Conference. The teams didn't meet again until the first round of 2018 when the Sharks feasted on the Ducks in four games, outscoring them 16-4.

5. When the Vegas Golden Knights entered the league, they ousted the Sharks in six games in the second round of the playoffs on their way to the Stanley Cup final. The teams met the following year in the first round and Vegas took a 3-1 lead in games. The Sharks forced Game 7 at home but trailed 3-0 midway through the third period. They then scored r goals to take the lead during a controversial major penalty to the Knights. Vegas tied the game with 47 seconds remaining only to see the Sharks win in overtime. The NHL later apologized to Vegas for the blown penalty call.

6. When it comes to points percentage, the Sharks have had the most regular-season success against the Winnipeg Jets and Washington Capitals, as of 2020. They had a 21-9-2-3 record against the Jets for a .671 percentage and a 28-13-1-3 mark against Washington for a .667 percentage.

7. The current NHL squads San Jose has faced over 20 times that give them the most trouble are the New York Rangers and Buffalo Sabres. They were 11-25-3-4 against the Rangers for a .337 percentage and were 12-22-4-5 against Buffalo for a .337 percentage.

8. The Sharks have played a total of 41 playoff series as of 2020 with a record of 20-21 for a .488 winning percentage; their won-lost record is 119-122. San Jose had played 15 different teams in the postseason with winning records against five of them, even records against five clubs and losing marks against another five squads.

9. The team San Jose has faced most in the playoffs is the St. Louis Blues; they have met six times with each team winning three series. The Sharks also have even playoff series records against Anaheim (1-1), Los Angeles (2-2), Vancouver (1-1), and Vegas (1-1).

10. The Sharks have winning playoff series records against Arizona (1-0), Calgary (2-1), Colorado (3-2), Detroit (3-2), and Nashville (3-0). They have losing records against Chicago (0-1), Dallas (0-3), Edmonton (0-2), Pittsburgh (0-1), and Toronto (0-1).

CHAPTER 15:

THE AWARDS SECTION

QUIZ TIME!

1. What was the first major trophy won by a member of the Sharks organization?

    a. Jack Adams Award
    b. NHL Foundation Player Award
    c. Calder Memorial Trophy
    d. Bill Masterton Memorial Trophy

2. Who was the first Sharks player named to the NHL All-Rookie Team in 1993-94?

    a. Mike Rathje
    b. Jeff Friesen
    c. Sandis Ozolinsh
    d. Viktor Kozlov

3. San Jose won its first President's Trophy in 2008-09.

    a. True
    b. False

4. Who was the first player chosen to represent the franchise in the NHL All-Star Game in 1992?

    a. Pat Falloon

    b. Kelly Kisio

    c. Doug Wilson

    d. Artūrs Irbe

5. How many points did the Sharks post when they won their first President's Trophy?

    a. 117

    b. 113

    c. 111

    d. 108

6. For which season did Brent Burns win the James Norris Memorial Trophy?

    a. 2014-15

    b. 2015-16

    c. 2016-17

    d. 2017-18

7. Which of the following players did not appear in the 2009 All-Star Game?

    a. Dan Boyle

    b. Patrick Marleau

    c. Devin Setoguchi

    d. Joe Thornton

8. Igor Larionov won the Frank J. Selke Trophy in his first season with the Sharks.

a. True

b. False

9. Who was named Sharks' Rookie of the Year by the organization in 2019-20?

   a. Noah Gregor

   b. Dylan Gambrell

   c. Radim Šimek

   d. Mario Ferraro

10. Which netminder won the Calder Memorial Trophy with San Jose?

   a. Vesa Toskala

   b. Thomas Greiss

   c. Evgeni Nabokov

   d. Aaron Dell

11. Vesa Toskala was the first Sharks goalie named to the NHL All-Rookie Team.

   a. True

   b. False

12. Which player won the organization's first-ever Media Good Guy Award in 2018-19?

   a. Tomas Hertl

   b. Joe Pavelski

   c. Logan Couture

   d. Brendan Dillon

13. How many All-Star Game appearances has Brent Burns made as of 2020?

a. 1

b. 2

c. 3

d. 4

14. Patrick Marleau once finished 3rd in voting for the Lady Byng Memorial Trophy.

    a. True

    b. False

15. Who was the first Sharks player to win a major NHL award?

    a. Tony Granato

    b. Artūrs Irbe

    c. Owen Nolan

    d. Joe Thornton

16. As of 2020, how many major NHL team and individual awards has the organization won?

    a. 15

    b. 10

    c. 13

    d. 9

17. The Maurice "Rocket" Richard Trophy was won by which player in 2005-06?

    a. Nils Ekman

    b. Patrick Marleau

    c. Jonathan Cheechoo

    d. Joe Thornton

18. Artūrs Irbe finished in what place in voting for the Vezina Trophy in the 1993-94 season?

    a. 3rd
    b. 4th
    c. 5th
    d. 6th

19. How many former Sharks have been inducted into the Hockey Hall of Fame as of 2020?

    a. 7
    b. 2
    c. 4
    d. 6

20. No Sharks player was selected for the 1998 All-Star Game.

    a. True
    b. False

QUIZ ANSWERS

1. D – Bill Masterton Memorial Trophy

2. B – Jeff Friesen

3. A – True

4. C – Doug Wilson

5. A – 117

6. C – 2016-17

7. C – Devin Setoguchi

8. B – False

9. D – Mario Ferraro

10. C – Evgeni Nabokov

11. B – False

12. D – Brendan Dillon

13. C – 3

14. A – True

15. A – Tony Granato

16. B – 10

17. C – Jonathan Cheechoo

18. C – 5th

19. D – 6

20. A – True

DID YOU KNOW?

1. As a franchise, the Sharks have captured several team and individual NHL awards as of 2020. They include the Presidents' Trophy (1), Clarence S. Campbell Bowl (1), Art Ross Trophy (1), Bill Masterton Memorial Trophy (1), Calder Memorial Trophy (1), Hart Memorial Trophy (1), James Norris Memorial Trophy (1), Lester Patrick Trophy (1), and the NHL Foundation Player Award (1).

2. The club has yet to win the Stanley Cup and no Sharks player has yet won the Vezina Trophy, William M. Jennings Award, Conn Smythe Trophy, Frank J. Selke Trophy, Ted Lindsay Award, Lady Byng Memorial Trophy, King Clancy Memorial Trophy, or the Mark Messier Leadership Award. Also, no coach has won the Jack Adams Award and no general manager has received the Jim Gregory General Manager of the Year Award.

3. Forward Joe Thornton led the NHL in scoring in 2005-06 and took home the Art Ross Trophy by notching 29 goals and 96 assists for 125 points. He tallied 9 goals and 24 assists in 23 contests with Boston and 20 goals and 72 assists in 58 games with San Jose; he was traded on Nov. 30, 2005. Thornton was the first player to win the Art Ross while playing with two teams in the same season.

4. The Hart Memorial Trophy is awarded to the player deemed most valuable to his team during the regular

season and is voted on by the media. The NHL Players' Association also takes its own vote and recognizes the season MVP with the Ted Lindsay Award. Forward Joe Thornton captured the Hart Trophy in 2006, the same year he won the Art Ross Trophy.

5. The Bill Masterton Trophy is awarded annually to the player who exemplifies perseverance, sportsmanship, and dedication to hockey. Forward Tony Granato won it in 1996-97, when he posted 25 goals and 40 points in 76 games. Granato was acquired before the season via a trade with Los Angeles and battled back to play after undergoing brain surgery earlier in 1996.

6. Brent Burns won the James Norris Trophy as the best defenseman in the league for the 2016-17 regular season. He scored 29 goals and 47 assists for 76 points that campaign and was also nominated for the Ted Lindsay Award for his exceptional play.

7. The Calder Memorial Trophy, awarded to the NHL's Rookie of the Year, went to goaltender Evgeni Nabokov for his play in 2000-01. The native of Kazakhstan went 32-21-7 in 66 games with a goals-against average of 2.19 and a .915 save percentage.

8. The only Sharks' player to lead the NHL in goals to win the Rocket Richard Trophy was forward Jonathan Cheechoo. He banged in a franchise-record 56 goals in 82 games in 2005-06 and also added 37 assists for a career-high 93 points. Cheechoo became the second aboriginal player to score more than 50 goals in a season that year.

9. Several Sharks have been chosen for NHL All-Star Teams. Goaltender Evgeni Nabokov made the First Team once. Defender Brent Burns has been selected to the First Team twice and the Second Team once. Defensemen Dan Boyle and Brian Campbell were each selected to the Second Team once. Left-winger Joe Pavelski once made the Second Team while center Joe Thornton has made the First Team once and Second Team twice.

10. Goaltender Evgeni Nabokov (2007-08), blue-liners Brad Stuart (1999-2000), Matt Carle (2006-07), and Marc-Edouard Vlasic (2006-07) and forwards Jeff Friesen (1994-95) and Logan Couture (2010-11) were all named to NHL All-Rookie Teams.

CONCLUSION

The San Jose Sharks have been chasing the Stanley Cup since 1991-92 and fans believe it won't be much longer now before they reach their goal.

The trivia and factbook you've just read deals with the franchise's history every step of the way from the 1991 NHL expansion and dispersal drafts right to the conclusion of the abbreviated 2019-20 NHL regular season.

The book contains a wide array of facts, trivia questions, and anecdotes about your favorite Sharks' players, coaches, and general managers.

Our goal was to serve up as much San Jose trivia as possible in a fun and lighthearted manner as fans are given the chance to relive the excitement and disappointment the franchise has delivered over the years.

We certainly hope it was an enjoyable way to reaffirm your knowledge of the team and perhaps learn something new at the same time.

With this much information at your fingertips, you'll be in a perfect position to prepare for the next trivia challenge or contest that comes your way from family members, friends, and fellow Shark supporters.

There is no doubt that San Jose Shark fans are among the loudest and most passionate in the world of sports as they stick by their team through thick and thin. We hope this book will be of some assistance the next time somebody challenges your knowledge of this fine organization.

Thanks for standing by the franchise and taking the time to read through its latest trivia and factbook.

Made in the USA
Coppell, TX
14 June 2021